The Last Man in Europe:

An Essay on George Orwell

By the same author

THE WHEEL OF EMPIRE *A Study of the Imperial Idea in Some Late Nineteenth and Early Twentieth-Century Fiction*

The Last Man in Europe

An Essay on George Orwell

Alan Sandison

BOOKS
10 East 53d St. New York 10022
(a division of Harper & Row Publishers, Inc.)

First published in the United Kingdom 1974 by
THE MACMILLAN PRESS LTD

Published in the U.S.A. 1974 by
HARPER & ROW PUBLISHERS, INC.
BARNES & NOBLE IMPORT DIVISION

ISBN–06–496075–7

*Photoset, printed and bound
in Great Britain*

PR6029
R98Z83

To my Mother and Father

Contents

Foreword

Because in what follows considerable stress is laid on a certain religious tradition it is perhaps desirable to make it clear that the writer is committed neither to it nor to any other religion. The object is not to suggest parallels for extrinsic uplift but to describe Orwell's fundamental moral sympathies, and in doing so to expose the nature of his creative vision and the impulse behind it.

I have to thank the University of Durham for defraying some of the expenses incurred in preparing this book for publication.

To my friend and former colleague, Myrddin Jones of the University of Exeter, I owe a debt of a different order. With characteristic generosity he has found time in a busy programme to read and discuss various drafts of this essay very much to the benefit of the author.

A.S.

Acknowledgements

The author and publishers are grateful to the following for permission to quote copyright material: Mrs Sonia Brownell Orwell; Brandt & Brandt, for extracts from *Nineteen Eighty-Four* (copyright 1949 by Harcourt, Brace & World, Inc.) and from *Down and Out in Paris and London* (Harcourt, Brace & World, Inc., copyright 1933 by George Orwell, renewed 1960 by Sonia Pitt-Rivers); Harcourt Brace Jovanovich, Inc. (United States publishers of *The Road to Wigan Pier, Keep the Aspidistra Flying, A Clergyman's Daughter* and *Such, Such Were the Joys*); and Martin Secker & Warburg Ltd.

1 To Prove all Things

Prove all things, hold fast that which is good
1 Thessalonians v. 21

When Martin Luther stubbornly refused to withdraw his criticism of the Church before the Imperial Diet at Worms in 1521, he was duly made aware of the extreme consequences to himself if he persisted in his recusancy. The warning was delivered by Johann von der Eck, Luther's interrogator before the Diet, who clearly saw himself not just as the secretary-representative of the Archbishop of Trier but as the oracle of a prescriptive and systematic absolutism established in the dogma of the Universal Church. To us today the importance of what this voice says – in von der Eck's own carefully edited account – is virtually equalled by how it says it: we are struck by the way it clarifies the contending ideologies, but we are perhaps even more struck by the familiarity of its vocabulary:

> Even granted that some of your books contain nothing harmful, a point that we do not concede; but cut out your pernicious and poisonous dogmas, cut out the blasphemous passages, cut out the heresies and what savours of heresy, cut out the passages hurtful to the Catholic faith; then no danger will arise from what is right and proper. His sacred and imperial Majesty is prepared to deal very leniently with these matters; and if you alter your views will prevail upon the supreme pontiff not to destroy and blot out the good with the bad. If, however, you obstinately persist in your notorious errors and heresies as up to the present, most certainly all memory of you will be wiped out, and everything, whether right or wrong, together with their author, will be condemned.[1]

To the language of totalitarianism Luther opposed a language of his own, empirical in every sense, and individualist. A fair if not particularly rich sample is to be found in his reply to von der Eck:

> Unless I am convinced by the testimony of Scripture or by plain reason (for I believe in neither the Pope nor in councils alone, for it is well known, not only that they have erred, but also have contradicted themselves), I am mastered by the passages of Scripture which I have quoted, and my conscience is captive to the word of God.[2]

But, though von der Eck's speech gave no inkling of it, the totalitarianism he enunciated was losing its substance. Luther, after all, did obstinately persist, and he was not blotted out. The profound internal deficiences of Church and Papacy invited contempt of their authority – seen perhaps in its most extreme political form when Charles V, the Holy Roman Emperor, responded to the Pope's unscrupulous intriguing against him by declaring war on the Papacy and sacking Rome in 1527. But though these circumstances allowed the emergence of Luther, and even, in the form of clerical abuses, supplied his motivation, for his wider impact he was drawing on and focusing the expanding energy released by what we call the Renaissance. Erik Erikson in his exceptionally stimulating study, *Young Man Luther*, argues that Luther could well be seen as undertaking the dirty work of the Renaissance 'by applying some of the individualistic principles immanent in the Renaissance to the Church's still highly fortified homeground – the conscience of ordinary man'. In this contention, Luther is found to have provided for the post-Renaissance world a new and workable morality. Certainly as Erikson puts it, the tools he used were those of the Renaissance:

> fervent return to the original texts, determined anthropocentrism (if in Christocentric form); and the affirmation of his own organ of genius and craftsmanship, namely, the voice of the vernacular.

What these tools were to fashion we can see foreshadowed in Luther's stand against authoritarianism in the name of 'plain reason' and personal judgement: or as we might say, empiricism and individualism. 'Prove all things' had been St Paul's forgotten exhortation to the Christians of Thessalonia, and in seizing upon it to defend his position, Luther found a motto not only for himself but for that moral and intellectual movement which was to exert, down to our own day, a major creative influence on the development of Western culture.

Critics have for some time sought to establish a satisfactory provenance for George Orwell so that his moral and creative vision could be more properly understood, but independence and variety rather than agreement characterise their solutions. Malcolm Muggeridge for example, in his introduction to *Burmese Days*, describes him as 'a throwback to the late Victorian days', while John Weightman reviewing the lately-published *The Collected Essays, Letters and Journalism of George Orwell*, suggests that his natural society is that of Samuel Johnson and the Augustans. In *The Crystal Spirit* (1967), George Woodcock places him somewhere between these two extremes as 'the last of a nineteenth-century tradition of individualist radicals which bred such men as Hazlitt, Cobbett and Dickens'. In a more recent work on Orwell *The Makings of George Orwell*, Keith Alldritt sees him as the dialectical product of his attraction to, and reaction against the *symbolistes*.

Placing Orwell in these different contexts is understandable and, as these writers have shown in varying degrees, defensible: his world-view does embrace elements characteristic of, say, Johnson and Swift, as well as Baudelaire and Kipling. But a chameleon on a tartan rug is still a chameleon and the necessity we remain under is that of discovering the basic shape or perspective which will allow these disparate elements to be seen as integral parts of a larger but quite distinct whole.

In fact it is arguable that those who have sought Orwell's provenance in these places have been over-ingenious or, at any rate, have sought for it through too narrow a focus. For few writers have been so very insistent in tracing their roots: indeed to a quite remarkable extent it is the subject of his books.

In his essay 'The Fiction of Anti-Utopia' Irving Howe

makes this excellent point:

> The idea of the personal self, which for us has become an indispensable assumption of existence, is seen by Zamiatin, Orwell and Huxley as a *cultural* idea. It is a fact within history, the product of the liberal era, and because it is susceptible to historical growth and decline, it may also be susceptible to historical destruction.[4]

To Orwell, much more than to the others, this realisation is creatively central to his works. At times it even becomes obsessive, and not surprisingly, for his deep and permanent anxiety about his own spiritual identity made it, to him, much more of a pressing, subjective concern.

Support for Howe's contention can be found in this passage in 'Literature and Totalitarianism':

> We live in an age in which the autonomous individual is ceasing to exist – or perhaps one ought to say, in which the individual is ceasing to have the illusion of being autonomous. Now in all that we say about literature, and (above all) in all that we say about criticism, we instinctively take the autonomous individual for granted. The whole of modern European literature – *I am speaking of the literature of the past four hundred years* – is built on the concept of intellectual honesty, or if you like to put it that way, on Shakespeare's maxim, 'to thine own self be true'.[5]

I have italicised the acknowledgement of the debt owed to the Renaissance and (as we shall see more explicitly) to the Reformation; but such references pervade his work for this is the perspective in which he sees himself as a man and as a writer. When he champions literature 'as we know it', he is asserting a moral doctrine of freedom of individual conscience and personal judgement: with the Reformation, as he saw it, the individual came of age. ('One cannot really be Catholic and grown up', he wrote in his notes for a book on Evelyn Waugh.) Consequently there can be no accommodation between totalitarianism and such a literature:

> . . . in any totalitarian society that survives for more than a couple of generations, it is probable that prose literature, of

the kind that has existed during the past four hundred years, must actually come to an end.[6]

Or even more uncompromisingly:

'Prose literature as we know it is the product of rationalism, of the Protestant centuries, of the autonomous individual'.[7]

Unequivocally Orwell accepts his place in the liberal-individualistic tradition of these four hundred years, consequently giving to his radicalism its strong conservative note. He is certainly for reform and change but from the dialectical position of the Protestant holding fast to his belief in the autonomous individual. Naturally this defines for him the nature of the enemy:

Why is it that everything we mean by culture is menaced by totalitarianism? Because totalitarianism menaces the existence of the individual, and the last four or five hundred years have put the individual so emphatically on the map that it is hard for us to imagine him off it again.[8]

Not only is Orwell's consciousness of the personal self as a cultural idea made perfectly clear here: so is his commitment to the defence of a concept once again vulnerable to the encroachment of totalitarianism. And it is his fidelity to this engagement that provides his work with consistency and unity, and his readers with a clear perspective within which to view his creative achievement.

It may be objected that to advance the Protestant tradition as Orwell's provenance is about as meaningful as to suggest the Garden of Eden as my own. Even at this early stage, however, the evidence of the extracts quoted might, in their specificity, give anyone pause before taking up such a position. They suggest what the rest of his work confirms that it is not enough simply to say that Orwell's thinking takes its colour from the Protestant tradition, or that he shares the cultural identity of the last four or five hundred (Protestant) years. Quite literally, Orwell *lives* in the dynamic – almost, one might say, in the original ideological ferment – of the tradition, seeing both his conscience and his individual consciousness depending upon it.

Agnostic as he formally is, he out-Protestants the Protestants in disregarding the institution and getting back to first principles, reviving and reasserting them with fundamentalist passion. Ultimately, however, fundamentalism is simply an admission of unpunctuality – an apology for not being there at the time, and Orwell is perfectly well aware of it. He knows that this great 'moment' which Luther did so much to precipitate has passed or is passing: hence not only the fundamentalism of his world-view but also its bleakness. Hence too his passion, for what he sees assailed by the regrouped forces of totalitarianism is not only the economic, social and political products of the old empirical tradition, but its moral product: that concept of self which derives from the individual's freedom to 'prove all things' and which like the tradition itself and its origins, is 'a fact within history' susceptible to growth, decline – and possibly even destruction. To Orwell, man and writer, this *sine qua non* is what is in deadly peril: it is this which he is fiercely determined to defend and it is this which is the subject of his writing.

But if his subject is the concept of the personal self and its welfare, it became so neither theoretically nor mythically. Refusing to see it as in any way separate or separable from its moral antecedents in the new dispensation secured for the individual by the Reformation, Orwell quite simply believed in it as a matter of profound faith. So that, to a quite unusual degree, in writing *about* his subject he is writing *from* it. There is no tendency to indulge in myth-making, nor to 'use' this faith structurally as, for example, Kipling deploys faith in society and custom to keep solipsism at bay.

Orwell's instinct is that of the *homo religiosus*: his particular source of moral and spiritual energy the Protestant dialectic. Critics of Orwell have neglected to see this for the rich matrix it is, and which, properly regarded, enables us to appreciate more fully the nature and the dynamic, as well as the unity, of his creative vision. The mind to which Orwell gives vivid expression – even the vocabulary itself – is, for all his avowed agnosticism, identifiable with those reformers who, in order to establish the individual's right to prove all things, broke from

the shelter of the Mother Church. With this historical difference: that Luther and von der Eck have changed places and it
is now the former upon whose empire the sun is going down.

2 Operating inside Nature

We need no proof of His identity nor of ours as long as, at any given time, an essential part of our equipment and a segment of His world continue to conform each other. This is the law of operating inside nature.

Erik Erikson

The law of operating inside nature which Erikson describes in *Young Man Luther* is a quite fundamental precept for Orwell; one on which depended his whole notion of the free personality. But what does nature really mean to him? It means, of course, the nature of rocks and stones and trees to which he would seem at first glance to have an almost sentimental attachment:

Sometimes on summer afternoons there were wonderful expeditions across the Downs to a village called Birling Gap, or to Beachy Head, where one bathed dangerously among the chalk boulders and came home covered with cuts . . . And there was the pleasure of keeping caterpillars – the silky green and purple puss-moth, the ghostly green poplar-hawk, the privet-hawk, large as one's third finger . . . and . . . there was the excitement of dredging the dew-ponds on the Downs for enormous newts with orange-coloured bellies.[1]

Despite the larger nostalgia lurking behind this, there is a real joy in nature, authenticated in the delight and precision of the observation and in the capacity to name. In a much earlier work, *Burmese Days*, the same response is in evidence:

There was a stirring high-up in the peepul tree, and a bubbling noise like pots boiling. A flock of green pigeons were up there, eating the berries. Flory gazed up into the great green dome of the tree, trying to distinguish the birds; they were invisible, they matched the leaves so perfectly, and yet the whole tree was alive with them, shimmering, as though the ghosts of birds were shaking it . . . Then a single green pigeon fluttered down and perched on a lower branch. It did not know that it was being watched. It was a tender thing, smaller than a tame dove, with jade-green back as smooth as velvet, and neck and breast of iridescent colours. Its legs were like the pink wax that dentists use.

There are a lot of literary echoes here, in particular from Kipling and Forster, but the same precise observation dominates the account and the last sentence is characteristically his. A little later in the same book comes another piece of description which has no moral significance for the tale whatsoever but is included simply because it is intrinsically interesting to the writer:

One does not often see green pigeons so closely when they are alive. They are high-flying birds, living in tree-tops, and they do not come to the ground, or only to drink. When one shoots them, if they are not killed outright, they cling to the branch until they die, and drop long after one has given up waiting and gone away.[2]

Orwell is obviously moved by nature and drawn to it; but he is also capable of looking at it with a scientific eye. There is nothing contradictory in this and certainly no very persuasive argument that his true provenance will be discovered in the society of the Pre-Romantics. However there is, nonetheless, a special significance in this particular combination of mind and sense.

Orwell's problem, reiterated time and again, is the loss of faith in immortality. Disbelieving in God, he nevertheless believes profoundly in the individual self; but bereft of the notion of immortality how is faith in the latter to be sustained? The answer lies principally in nature. If the divinity of scripture no longer carries conviction there is still a scripture-in-nature to which Orwell offers a remarkable devotion. In a letter to Henry Miller, he writes:

. . . I have a sort of belly-to-earth attitude and always feel

uneasy when I get away from the ordinary world where
grass is green, stones hard, etc.[3]

Though it is deliberately understated here, this interplay –
even interdependence – of material world and man's senses is
absolutely vital to Orwell's creed and as such conspicuously
informs every book he wrote. In an essay written towards the
end of his life he manages to sound almost whimsical about it,
yet all the while he is being sharply explicit:

So long as I remain alive and well I shall continue to feel
strongly about prose style, to love the surface of the earth,
and to take pleasure in solid objects and scraps of useless
information.[4]

Nature, in the sense of the surface of the earth, is *real*. Its reality
is conveyed to the individual through his senses and in
precisely this commerce is his personal identity confirmed.
For the senses are inalienable and in the reception of their
independent and particular report of the natural world is
proof of individuality. Not that they are the sum of personality
which to Orwell is something much more spiritual than that
would allow as we shall see when we come to discuss the
almost equal importance of history to the individual; but on
the evidence of the senses operating in nature the entity of the
self exists and is able to make personal judgements and establish personal values. Consequently, the greatest moral danger
Orwell can envisage for man is that he should be denied contact with the ordinary world where grass is green, stones hard.
Very much as Erikson describes the process in the quotation
at the head of this chapter the reality of the natural world and
individual identity confirm each other through the medium of
the senses.

Interestingly, at that point in his book Erikson is describing
the disciplined sensuality of the Renaissance:

Renaissance sensuality . . . tried to make the body an intui-
tive and disciplined tool of reality: it did not permit the
body to be sickened with sinfulness, nor the mind to be
chained to a dogma; it insisted on a full interplay between
man's senses and intuitions and the world of appearances,
facts, and laws.[5]

Orwell's insistence is of a similar order though with a post-Lutheran additive which ensures that what is a statement of moral principle will not be seen simply as an aesthetic theory (to him, of course, no divorce between the two is conceivable since he regards aesthetic and moral considerations as inextricable) and also predicates a new consciousness of sin. Man's care is to live in this direct and honest confrontation, faithful to the evidence of his senses: what sight and touch seize upon as solid objects must be truth. Orwell would, one feels, have agreed entirely with Leonardo da Vinci's assertion that 'mental things which have not gone through the senses are vain and bring forth no truth except detrimental'.[6] In *Coming Up for Air*, that lesser mortal George Bowling is made to challenge people to recognise the pleasure and the value in sense-impressions, now being neglected with ominous implications for his world-view. Characteristic of both himself and his author is the stress he lays on 'the feeling of wonder' liberated by such contact with nature:

> Farther down the hedge the pool was covered with duck-weed, so like a carpet that if you didn't know what duck-weed was you might think it was solid and step on it. I wondered why it is that we're all such bloody fools. Why don't people instead of the idiocies they do spend their time on, just walk round *looking* at things? That pool, for instance – all the stuff that's in it. Newts, water-snails, water-beetles, caddis-flies, leeches, and God knows how many other things that you can only see with a microscope. The mystery of their lives, down there under the water. You could spend a life-time watching them, ten life-times, and still you wouldn't have got to the end even of that one pool. And all the while the sort of feeling of wonder, the peculiar flame inside you. It's the only thing worth having, and we don't want it.[7]

The result of the direct interplay between man's senses and the world of appearances, facts, and laws – nature – is the same for Orwell as for the Renaissance: the confirmation of the reality and scope of the individual self – and access to the empirical method. The word 'direct' is, of course, of the greatest importance. No Pope, nor his Orwellian equivalent, the Party, is to come between man and his scripture-in-nature: nothing must be allowed to obstruct the operation of that 'rational, sceptical experimental habit of mind', the acquisition of which, as 'a method that can be used on any problem one meets . . . a way of looking at the world', was for Orwell the true definition of a scientific education.[8] So long as one holds fast to the idea of an external reality obeying certain natural laws and verifiable by the senses, one has a chance of defending that inner light against any totalitarian attempt to extinguish it. Such a reality is proof that, after all, everything does *not* happen in the mind: a reassurance of great comfort when confronted by manipulators like O'Brien with their vast power based on a very different proposition. *The Theory and Practice of Oligarchical Collectivism* – Goldstein's book – puts it very succinctly:

> The empirical method of thought, on which all the scientific achievements of the past were founded, is opposed to the most fundamental principles of Ingsoc.[9]

Thus to permit the infringement of the individual's right to act on the evidence of his senses, or to allow the violation of the natural laws, or to deny objective reality, was to open the door wide to totalitarianism:

> The atom bombs are piling up in the factories, the police are prowling through the cities, the lies are streaming from the loudspeakers, but the earth is still going round the sun, and neither the dictators nor the bureaucrats, deeply as they disapprove of the process, are able to prevent it.[10]

But even in 1939 Orwell was conceding that the 'peculiar horror of the present moment' was that one could no longer be sure that in the long run 'common-sense' would win against the totalitarians: 'It is quite possible that we are descending into an age in which two and two will make five when the leader says so'.[11] In *Nineteen Eighty-Four* two and two do make five and the sun goes round the earth.

Nature to Orwell is a sort of moral gold-standard. To abandon it is not only to debase the spiritual life but to de-stroy the very currency of the personal self. His premises, he acknowledges, are ultimately derived from the achievements of the Renaissance and the Reformation, which the succeeding 'four to five hundred years' have consolidated by putting the individual 'so emphatically on the map that it is hard for us to imagine him off it again'. His goal is still identifiable with that of the new dispensation: a *free* interplay of sense and material world, and freedom of conscience in drawing conclusions. If in this the reformationists saw the means of spiritual and moral salvation, so too did Orwell and in a sense only slightly modified. He would certainly have understood and sympathised with the brisk summary of the position by his contemporary W.II. Auden, when the latter concluded that '. . . the laws of nature to which, whether he likes it or not, [man] must conform are of divine origin'.[12] For in nature Orwell discovered laws which not only helped to verify his own being but also formed and guaranteed the individual's moral sense. In the absence of a transcendental divinity nature is now the last and dangerously brittle means of defending the individual and individual responsibility: the last stage for Orwell in that process which, he tells us repeatedly, began 'four or five hundred years ago'. Indeed, we can see limned in his emphasis on operating in nature much the same objectives and moral concern which shaped the Reformation in its earlier days. Erikson rehearses these in a way that points the comparison:

> For a little while Luther, this first revolutionary individualist, saved the Saviour from the tiaras and the ceremonies, the hierarchies and the thought-police, and put him back where he arose: in each man's soul.[13]

*   *   *

Why Orwell attached so much importance to operating inside nature may now be clearer, but there are many ramifications to this concern which invite exploration.

Nature is not of course simply the world of rocks and stones and trees plus the law of gravity: it is Wigan, the slums of London and Paris; it is a revolutionary (in more senses than one) *bordello* in Barcelona with a new poster requesting clients to 'please treat the ladies like comrades'. In other words it is everything which in its physicality is capable of making an impact on the senses. This dictates a focus narrowed to the concrete and within which, in the more fundamentalist Protestant tradition, man makes his soul. But Orwell outbids the Protestants in his passionate concern with physical environment and the individual: to him, they have, after all, only each other. (Or so it is made to appear: through the exertions of the five senses, a sixth, moral sense, is kept in such lively trim that we readily overlook the obscurity of its origins.)

Consequently we get a focus on 'the surface of the earth' so close that at times it is almost obsessive and the cumulative effect of this intense concentration on the physicality of environment becomes suffocating. The 'thingery' of this world assumes Brobdingnagian dimensions and all but overwhelm us: hair-cracks in ceilings become ravines with our moral selves tottering on the brink, and huge, voracious bugs scale the broken plaster with the predatory vigour of mountain-lions. An aspidistra shoots up to become a totem-pole of enviable potency, and a hotel is transformed into a great steam-engine shuddering in a fine frenzy, a miracle of machinery and intricate timing which grinds up the whole complex *danse macabre* of *patron, maître d'hôtel, chef du personnel,* waiters, laundresses, sewing women, *plongeurs,* and *cafetiers:*

> He led me down a winding staircase into a narrow passage, deep underground, and so low that I had to stoop in places. It was stiflingly hot and very dark, with only dim, yellow bulbs several yards apart. There seemed to be miles of dark labyrinthine passages – actually, I suppose, a few hundred yards in all – that reminded one queerly of the lower decks of a liner; there were the same heat and cramped space and warm reek of food, and a humming, whirring noise (it came from the kitchen furnaces) just like the whir of engines. We passed doorways which let out sometimes a shouting of oaths, sometimes the red glare of a fire, once a shuddering draught from an ice chamber. As we went along, something struck me violently in the back. It was a hundred-pound block of ice, carried by a blue-aproned porter. After him came a boy with a great slab of veal on his shoulder, his cheek pressed into the damp, spongy flesh. They shoved me aside with a cry of '*Sauve-toi, idiot!*' and rushed on.[14]

Down and Out in Paris and London is a sufficiently complex and interesting work to require much more detailed examination in a later chapter. However in the context of the present discussion it is worth noting that it is largely because of Orwell's preoccupation with the surface of the earth that the first section of the book is a failure. And something more, perhaps, for ultimately we feel cheated. There has been so much assurance that we are really going to meet life in the raw and learn what it is like where poverty and starvation are a man's only faithful companions. But instead of the penetrating insight into human experience which such a programme might be thought likely to offer, all we get is a mannered, highly literary, fiction: a series of 'vignettes' in the style of de Maupassant, and, of course, a feast of husks in a prodigality of sounds, sights, tastes and smells. In the end we know nothing of moral significance about the lives of the people who swarm in this wretched quarter. We only know that they *do* swarm; that they live and work in disagreeable conditions and that they frequently die of malnutrition and associated complaints. Orwell has, very literally, confined himself to the surface of the earth and become, simply, superficial; concealing his lack of substance with an overdose of form. The account remains, for all its observation, that of an earnest 'slummer'. There is something appallingly insensitive in his description of himself, now baled out of his 'condition of poverte' (as the epigraph self-consciously has it) by the ever-willing B, putting on his best suit and returning to drink at the Auberge where he had worked amongst those genuinely trapped by their circumstances. It is very cool of him to sum up his visit with the casual remark that 'It is a curious sensation, being a customer where you have been a slave's slave'.[15]

On the evidence of the first section of the book it is tempting to see Orwell as the Kipling of the Left Bank – except that it would do some injustice to Kipling. At least the latter's sensitivity would not have allowed him to go back to the Auberge – far less to write about having done so – and something of his deeper sympathy would have emerged in his treatment of those shut in their treadmill. Nevertheless, there is a similar slickness in the vignettes and a superficiality which Kipling

was certainly capable of, even if it was often carefully cultivated. Other significant characteristics which they share are also
strongly in evidence here. Kipling, too, had the true Protestant
tradition in his blood (almost literally; both his grandfathers
were Methodist ministers: against this, Orwell could have
mustered a paternal grandfather who, after serving in the
Indian Army, became an Anglican clergyman), and his admiration for the man bent to the task which lies nearest to hand
is paralleled in Orwell's regard for the hotel-workers taking 'a
genuine pride in their work, beastly and silly though it is. If a
man idles, the others soon find him out, and conspire against
him to get him sacked.'[16] It will become clear later why Orwell
so readily identified himself with the idiom and the ethos of
the group currently being cultivated.

There is the same pleasure taken in being part of a large,
efficient machine in which every man has a firmly-allocated
task:

> In a hotel a huge and complicated machine is kept running
> by an inadequate staff, because every man has a well-
> defined job and does it scrupulously.[17]

Perhaps above all this there is the 'knowingness' so typical of
Kipling. This is not just there in the presumption lying behind
the glib thumb-nail sketching of humanity but in their readi-
ness of both writers to claim for themselves a worldly expertise
in which they take a fledgling's – an owlish fledgling's – pride:

> Six francs is a shilling, and you can live on a shilling a day
> in Paris if you know how. But it is a complicated business.[18]

or:

> The thing that would astonish anyone coming for the first
> time into the service quarters of a hotel would be the fearful
> noise and disorder during the rush hours. It is something so
> different from the steady work in a shop or a factory that it
> looks at first sight like sheer bad management. But it is
> really quite unavoidable, and for this reason. . . .[19]

or (of meat which has passed through many hands on its way
to the dining-room):

> Whenever one pays more than, say, ten francs for a dish of

meat in Paris, one may be certain that it has been fingered in this manner.[20]

These are the remarks of a would-be worldly insider, of someone who knows the ropes, and as such they have an obvious affinity with an observation like this:

> One of the few advantages that India has over England is a great knowability. After five years' service a man is directly or indirectly acquainted with the two or three hundred Civilians in his province, all the Messes of ten or twelve Regiments and Batteries, and some fifteen hundred other people of the non-official caste. In ten years his knowledge should be doubled, and at the end of twenty he knows, or knows something about, every Englishman in the Empire, and may travel anywhere and everywhere without paying hotel-bills.[21]

In both cases there is less in this protested mastery of their environment than meets the eye. There is no doubt, however, that physical activity in an exceptionally physical world was of great moral importance to both writers, though in Kipling's bleaker and more cynical vision it tended to become little more than an expedient verifying self-consciousness.

The unrelenting pressure of the material world upon the reader, deriving from Orwell's at times almost desperate faith in nature, is also felt strongly in *The Road to Wigan Pier*. Of course the whole concern of the book is with the surface of the earth but, that allowed, nobody would mistake it for a 'Report on Working-class Conditions in Wigan'. It is, as its highly allusive and suggestive title itself declares – the road *back* from Mandalay, with all that that might imply of guilt or penitence – a carefully and even subtly-wrought literary structure designed to incorporate and project aspects of experience and a personal vision not found in the average Blue Book. Orwell thus sets up for himself here another god in addition to Kipling's God of Things as they Are, and his representation of the surface of the earth is leavened by his more abstract concern with his (or his protagonist's) moral condition. *The Road to Wigan Pier* is to be judged as an aesthetic whole in which a very personal and quite nonfactual element is heavily involved.

The first part of the book suffers considerably on this cri-
terion simply because of the stress on physicality. The 'clumping of the mill-girls' clogs down the cobbled street' in the first
paragraph is menacing enough but the avalanche that waits us
in the next is all but overwhelming:

> Years earlier the house had been an ordinary dwelling-
> house, and when the Brookers had taken it and fitted it out
> as a tripe-shop and lodging-house, they had inherited some
> of the more useless pieces of furniture and had never had
> the energy to remove them. We were therefore sleeping in
> what was still recognizably a drawing-room. Hanging from
> the ceiling there was a heavy glass chandelier on which the
> dust was so thick that it was like fur. And covering most of
> one wall there was a huge hideous piece of junk, something
> between a sideboard and a hall-stand, with lots of carving
> and little drawers and strips of looking-glass, and there was
> a once-gaudy carpet ringed by the slop-pails of years, and
> two gilt chairs with burst seats, and one of those old-
> fashioned horsehair armchairs which you slide off when you
> try to sit on them. The room had been turned into a
> bedroom by thrusting four squalid beds in among this other
> wreckage.[22]

The stern refusal to avert his eyes from anything at all, continually threatens to crowd us out – whether it is Mr. Brooker
'carrying a full chamber pot which he gripped with the thumb
well over the rim', or the crumbs which the narrator got to
know by sight, watching their 'progress up and down the table
from day to day'. Relief and sympathy follow the narrator's
decision to abandon the Brookers' house, tinged with respect
for his fortitude and moderation:

> On the day when there was a full chamber-pot under the
> breakfast table I decided to leave. The place was beginning
> to depress me.[23]

But the persistent detail is not left behind with it:

> I notice that the Rev. W.R. Inge, in his book *England*,
> accuses the miners of gluttony. From my own observation I

should say that they eat astonishingly little. Most of the miners I stayed with ate slightly less than I did. Many of them declare that they cannot do their day's work if they have had a heavy meal beforehand, and the food they take with them is only a snack, usually bread-and-dripping and cold tea. They carry it in a flat tin called a snapcan which they strap to their belts.[24]

It is another of the consequences of the too-close focus that all too frequently the bed-pan only gives way to the deadpan; except, that is, when they choose to lie down together.

Orwell's interest in physical detail and hard facts is often indulged with a conspicuous lack of literary tact; but in his emphasis on this stratum of reality, as in the defence of his whole order of which it is something like the foundation, he feels himself to be fighting a rear-guard action. Nature, 'the world of appearances, facts, and laws', morally so essential to him, is being subverted, and not least by those who would seek to asperse 'facts' concrete or abstract:

> In the past people deliberately lied, or they unconsciously coloured what they wrote, or they struggled after the truth, well knowing that they must make many mistakes; but in each case they believed that 'the facts' existed and were more or less discoverable.[25]

But that was in the past: now, as he shows most powerfully in *Nineteen Eighty-Four*, 'facts' are there to be manipulated in the interests of the ruling party, and the sort of detail he recounts so meticulously and affectionately in *The Road to Wigan Pier* are the vestigial remains of the road we have travelled 'for the last three or four hundred years', and the culture we had built upon it. The documentary style itself which allows such attention to detail is very much part of the defence he is conducting, at once a product of the 'surface of the earth' philosophy, and its propagandist. 'The truth is', he wrote in a review of Miller's *Black Spring*, 'that the written word loses its power if it departs too far, or rather if it stays away too long, from the ordinary world where two and two make four'.[26] If occasionally his failure to depart far enough damages his art, at least it bears witness to the urgency of his moral concern.

But though Orwell's over-investment in 'solid objects' can become an unbalanced passion and lead to real weakness in his writing, properly tempered it can be a source of strength. As a whole *The Road to Wigan Pier* is not a failure because he does succeed in introducing perspective as the book unfolds. Even in the earlier section there is the haunting image of the young women kneeling in a back-yard poking a stick up a waste-pipe in an effort to clear it:

> She looked up as the train passed, and I was almost near enough to catch her eye. She had a round pale face, the usual exhausted face of the slum girl who is twenty-five and looks forty, thanks to miscarriages and drudgery; and it wore, for the second in which I saw it, the most desolate, hopeless expression I have ever seen. . . . She knew well enough what was happening to her – understood as well as I did how dreadful a destiny it was to be kneeling there in the bitter cold, on the slimy stones of a slum backyard, poking a stick up a foul drain-pipe.[27]

The account gains its effect not from the concrete detail by itself – 'her sacking apron, her clumsy clogs, her arms reddened by the cold', but because that is observed through the window of the train carrying the narrator away. However concrete and physical this act, it is beyond the reach of the observer, separated as the two are by the glass partition and the moving vehicle. Yet in their humanity, they are rightfully part of each other: though, equally, it seems to be inherent in their human condition that they should remain isolated from each other and so unfulfilled. It is a graphic description of the polar opposite of that intimacy for which Orwell, as we shall see, strove so hard; the antithesis, for example of that moment of communion with the militiaman in *Homage to Catalonia*. The train draws away and the woman is left there, sealed in, suffocatingly, in the coarse physicality of her personal world. The perspective widens as the distance between them grows, enlarging her predicament and its pathos. Of such a situation Thomas Carlyle wrote:

> Isolation   is   the   sum-total   of   wretchedness   to
> man . . . Encased each as in his transparent 'ice-palace'; our

brother visible in his, making signals and gesticulations to us; – visible, but forever unattainable: on his bosom we shall never rest, nor he on ours. It was not a God that did this; no![28]

It is worth noting that the description of the girl at the drain-pipe so superior to the clottedly factual writing referred to earlier, is quite deliberate art. Orwell did not, of course, invent the young woman, but according to his entry in the diary where he made notes of his experiences in preparation for the book, he comes across her while 'passing up a horrible squalid side-alley'.[29]

Later in the same book there is the impressive account of 'the scrambling for coal', which unlike the vignettes of life in Paris really does succeed in focusing the life of the community he is describing. It is a scene physical enough in all conscience but also full of action and Orwell is obliged to stand back and be selective. Not for the only time the sharply observed physicality of things balanced by a laconic reporter's voice recalls Swift:

Even at the bend the train was making twenty miles an hour. The men hurled themselves upon it, caught hold of the rings at the rear of the trucks and hoisted themselves up by way of the bumpers, five or ten of them on each truck. The driver took no notice. He drove up to the top of the slag-heap, uncoupled the trucks, and ran the engine back to the pit, presently returning with a fresh string of trucks. There was the same wild rush of ragged figures as before. In the end only about fifty men had failed to get on either train.

We walked up to the top of the slag-heap. The men were shovelling the dirt out of the trucks, while down below their wives and children were kneeling, swiftly scrabbling with their hands in the damp dirt and picking out lumps of coal the size of an egg or smaller. You would see a woman pounce on a tiny fragment of stuff, wipe it on her apron, scrutinise it to make sure it was coal, and pop it jealously into her sack . . .

This business of robbing the dirt trains takes place every day in Wigan, at any rate in winter, and at more collieries

than one. It is of course extremely dangerous. No one was
hurt the afternoon I was there, but a man had had both his
legs cut off a few weeks earlier, and another man lost several
fingers a week later.[30]

The powerful effect Orwell gets from juxtaposing the horror of
the bare facts with the dispassionate tone is very much that of
his admired Swift ('Our greatest prose writer') as is his achievement of the simultaneous effect of familiarity and distance in
his description of the woman who would 'pounce on a tiny
fragment of the stuff, wipe it on her apron, scrutinise it to
make sure it was coal, and pop it jealously into her sack.' Perhaps it is too successful for it naturally reminds us of the
Yahoos and their diamonds. On the other hand Orwell's purpose here is similar to Swift's, if less complex; for both want to
rouse readers actively to look at the truth, to strip the film of
familiarity and customary acceptance from the facts. The
subtle modulation of the authorial voice is not, however, uniform throughout the episode. The beginning, for instance, is
too flatly documentary:

> In Wigan the competition among unemployed people for
> the waste coal has become so fierce that it has led to an
> extraordinary custom called 'scrambling for the coal' which
> is well worth seeing. Indeed I rather wonder that it has
> never been filmed.[31]

It would be agreeable to think that the last sentence is an
attempt at the Swiftian poise ('Last week I saw a woman
flayed . . .') to shock us into indignation, but it is more likely
to be taken at its poker-face value. Of course there is much
more than this to be said about *The Road to Wigan Pier*, in particular about the role of the so-called narrator, but its place is
later.

'Operating in nature' as exclusively as Orwell wants to,
leads to a hyperconsciousness of the individual's physical
environment which at worst leaves the reader stumbling
across a landscape littered with solid objects. There is nothing
in the least abstract or Fichtean about this nature either no
self postulating non-self in order to have something to rebound
from into a definition of selfconsciousness. As in other matters

Orwell is quite fundamental in this: objective nature is real *not* illusory, verifiable by the senses and the senses alone. Only because nature exists objectively can our senses affirm themselves as organs of a personal self, which possesses, in consequence, the capacity to reach and sustain individual judgement, and asserts the freedom of the individual conscience.

The roots of this faith of Orwell's are quite clear. The Renaissance in promoting the view of man as, in Ficino's words, 'the centre of nature' set unparalleled store by individual talents and endowments. These in their various manifestations were the means of measuring all things. To Leonardo the trained eye was the supreme discoverer of nature's secrets; to Michaelangelo it was the hand guided by the intellect. As Erikson points out, such a view 'anchors the human identity in the hierarchy of organs and functions of the human body'.[32]

Orwell, too, effects just such an anchorage, clarifying still further his line of descent. But he shows the strain such a system entailed for a later generation bereft of the Renaissance's expansive vision. In his evolution, the nature-senses-self continuum has been reduced to an uncompromising spareness with the not unpredictable result that Orwell occasionally appears to be imprisoned in a cramped and airless space. Each of the components in the continuum acquires, as we have seen in discussing nature, a special intensity which can be both a strength and a weakness in the creative product. In the same way, the senses, so much a means of salvation get an emphasis which at times distorts the writer's response, and then again, duly moderated, can appear as a source of vitality. Often, his is not a 'disciplined sensuality', or at any rate, his submission to sense-impressions is not disciplined enough. His notorious over-reference to bad smells is the obvious example: so obvious that we easily overlook how evocative his writing is of the other four. The great importance of the visual sense has been underlined earlier in this section in discussing the immense pressure of the physical world, a pressure which is initially transmitted visually. But both aural and tactile senses are also very much involved, and there is at least one outstanding occasion when taste is used to sum up the degeneration of society:

The frankfurter had a rubber skin, of course, and my tem-
porary teeth weren't much of a fit. I had to do a kind of
sawing movement before I could get my teeth through the
skin. And then suddenly – pop! The thing burst in my
mouth like a rotten pear. A sort of horrible soft stuff was
oozing all over my tongue. But the taste! For a moment I
just couldn't believe it. Then I rolled my tongue round it
again and had another try. It was fish! A sausage, a thing
calling itself a frankfurter, filled with fish! I got up and
walked straight out without touching my coffee. God knows
what that might have tasted of.[33]

However if it is not quite true that smells dominate the other
sense-impressions, the incidence of *disagreeable* smells is conspicuous. There were several reasons for this and one of the
most important is the self-sufficient, hermetic nature of the
continuum of nature-sense-self whereby the activity of the
senses is intensified to such a degree that the stifling limita-
tions of these seen as a method of salvation declare themselves.
(We might notice in passing the relevance here of such titles as
Coming Up for Air and *Inside the Whale*.) The impression this conveys is of Orwell being trapped by a method of salvation he
abhors; finding himself not just in nature's bosom but,
because of his faith, jammed, Gulliver-like, with his face in
nature's pores. (This comparison with Swift could go further
here if we reflect for a moment on the latter's obsession with
ordure.) He dare not let the air in between the senses and the
nature they feed upon yet that nature *is* material and corrupt,
and, arguably, what his sense of smell gives him is a constant
reminder of corruptibility and in particular of his own corruption in such reliance upon sense. 'I smell because of my own
argument', says John Osborne's Luther when the disillu-
sioned Knight complains that he has been so close to him for
so long that he is even beginning to smell like him; 'I smell
because I never stop disputing with him . . .'.[34] Orwell too, in
this sense, smells because of his own argument.

It is a natural characteristic of the reformist doctrine which
stressed the individual's capacity to work his own salvation
free from external mediation that it gave prominence to the
activity of the senses; and more, that that activity tended to

get out of hand, giving undue prominence to 'the hierarchy of organs and functions of the human body'. Luther himself is perhaps the best example. Acutely, one might say sublimely, conscious of smells and well aware that a bad smell was, traditionally, a property of the devil, he rationalised the pleasure he took in them by seeing this as a means whereby he could out-Satan Satan. In the demonology of his day the devil could be routed if only one could contrive to fart in his face, a homeopathic remedy which Luther practised with great energy for most of his life. Perhaps Orwell lacked the degree of objectivity or the objectifying myth necessary to sort things out this far; at any rate for him smells excite a confused mixture of aversion and fascination.

In all this concern with nature the object, and with senses the medium, there is never any forgetting of the dominant subject: individual man. Operating within nature is the means whereby the individual achieves the realisation and fulfilment of the personal self. Supported morally by nothing but this interplay of sense and the world of appearances, facts and laws, Orwell's individual has a nobility and stature which if bleaker and less glamorous than his Renaissance original has an almost equal consciousness of what it costs. The austerity in this rendering of the humanist ethic with its heavy emphasis on contact with the physical world, identifies both itself and its provenance quite unequivocally in the essay 'Reflections on Gandhi'. Questioning the other worldly and anti-humanist implications of the mahatma's doctrines, Orwell writes:

> . . . Gandhi's teachings cannot be squared with the belief that Man is the measure of all things, and that our job is to make life worth living on this earth, which is the only earth we have. They make sense only on the assumption that God exists and that the world of solid objects is an illusion to be escaped from.[35]

In the early phase of the 'liberal culture we have lived in since the Renaissance'[36] individualism had to be fought for with the formidable hosts of the dogmatists, but in that seminal epoch it felt itself imbued with such immense and unexploited energy that against the ordained and apparently static position of the Church its dynamic was irresistible. There was still the Inquisition and the stake but the prize was clearly in sight: indeed, according to Pico della Mirandola, already in man's grasp:

> To him it is granted to have whatever he chooses, to be whatever he wills. On man when he came to life, the Father conferred the seeds of all kinds and the germs of every way of life . . . who would not admire this chameleon?[37]

Then the notion of the individual self was an expanding one: now, in Orwell, it is contracting and defensive, pessimistically waiting the final onslaught of the re-grouped dogmatists. The difference is summed up in the contrast between Pico della Mirandola's ecstatic vision of man newly liberated and the spareness of Orwell's grim, last-ditch stand enunciated by Winston Smith: 'Freedom is the freedom to say that two plus two make four'. At such moments of ideological crisis a fundamentalism reappears and here the concept of individualism means something fresh and powerful just because, as it was in the beginning, the cost is as clear as the penalty for failure.

So having restored to the concept something of its pristine force, Orwell can write with palpable sympathy and understanding on such unrewarding subjects as the irrational diet of the workless:

> When you are unemployed, which is to say when you are underfed, harassed, bored, and miserable, you don't *want* to eat dull wholesome food. You want something a little bit 'tasty'. There is always some cheaply pleasant thing to tempt you. Let's have three pennorth of chips! Run out and buy us a twopenny ice-cream! Put the kettle on and we'll all have a nice cup of tea! *That* is how your mind works when you are at the P.A.C. level. White bread-and-marg and sugared tea don't nourish you to any extent, but they are nicer (at least most people think so) than brown bread-and-dripping and cold water. Unemployment is an endless misery that has got to be constantly palliated, and especially with tea, the Englishman's opium. A cup of tea or even an aspirin is much better as a temporary stimulant than a crust of brown bread.[38]

In the same vein, he goes on to champion those who, instead of hoarding their pennies and facing the drab reality of their workless state, squander what little they have on appearances:

> The youth who leaves school at fourteen and gets a blind-alley job is out of work at twenty, probably for life; but for two pounds ten on the hire-purchase he can buy himself a suit which, for a little while and at a little distance, looks as though it had been tailored in Savile Row. The girl can look like a fashion plate at an even lower price. You may have three halfpence in your pocket and not a prospect in the world, and only the corner of a leaky bedroom to go home to; but in your new clothes you can stand on the street corner, indulging in a private daydream of yourself as Clark Gable or Greta Garbo, which compensates for a great deal.[39]

It is no great extravagance to see this as the instinctive human-ism of Shakespeare's

> Allow not nature more than nature needs,
> Man's life is cheap as beast's.

Even so, Orwellian man travels light: inevitably, for he cannot allow the infringement of his independence by any creeping institutionalism which would come to circumscribe his free-dom of response. Put another way, there must be no fatal ero-sion of the individual's moral identity in the interests of establishing the super-identity of a vast collectifying organism. Kipling expressed the same problem very succinctly in his rather desperate attempt to establish an economy of the self:

> For the eternal question still is whether the profit of any concession that a man makes to his Tribe, against the light that is in him, outweighs or justifies his disregard for that light.[40]

Orwell, however, frequently sounds even less willing to com-promise and while Kipling deeply fears loneliness, Orwell accepts it as the true penitent does his hair-shirt, as the inevit-able price for the salvation of the personal self. Individualism has to be fought for not once but continuously. If Luther put Christ back where he belongs in each man's soul Orwell recognised that to keep him there meant continuous rebellion.

Following the example of Luther who had praised radical suspiciousness as a guarantor of man's 'work, sense and reason', he explicitly preached the necessity of discontent. 'Certainly we ought to be discontented' he writes in 'Some Thoughts on the Common Toad': by being so we ensure that the revolutionary idea does not lose its dynamic, that we shall not have our conscience subverted, and that the all-important senses do not become blunted as he insists they had done in the case of a distinguished Victorian novelist whose 'discontent healed itself and he reverted to type'.[41] The loneliness inherent in this embattled stand, the affinity with Lutheran precept, above all the full consciousness of the antecedents of his position, find collective expression in this passage from 'The Prevention of Literature':

> . . . throughout the Protestant centuries, the idea of rebellion and the idea of intellectual integrity were mixed up. A heretic – political, moral, religious or aesthetic – was one who refused to outrage his own conscience. His outlook was summed up in the words of the Revivalist hymn:
>
> > Dare to be a Daniel,
> > Dare to stand alone;
> > Dare to have a purpose firm,
> > Dare to make it known.
>
> To bring this hymn up to date one would have to add a 'Don't' at the beginning of each line. For it is the peculiarity of our age that the rebels against the existing order, at any rate the most numerous and characteristic of them, are also rebelling against the idea of individual integrity. 'Daring to stand alone' is ideologically criminal as well as practically dangerous.[42]

The constant reference to nothing but one's own sense-experience and one's own conscience may leave one the freedom to recognise and resist those blandishments which would subvert one's independence but there is a high price to pay in terms of moral isolation from the human community, which no amount of 'commitment' will disguise. Nothing could be more obvious than Orwell's commitment – except his near-total failure at communion. 'It does not matter how small a cubicle is, the important thing is that a man should be alone when he sleeps'.[43] The remark is an absurd one: the voice of a sententious adolescent; but it is sad too, for through it speaks a man who could never be anything else but alone, waking or sleeping.

The isolation of the individual now ploughing his own very lonely furrow is a well known characteristic of reformation thinking and writing. But at least for such there was always God who would understand and might show mercy. Orwell's world was without this dimension and his loneliness was all the more stark – until, in one of the most spiritually despairing books in modern English literature, this dimension came back in the form of Divine Wrath.

3 A Laborious Calling

> Now, as I said, the way to the Celestial City lies just through this town, where this lusty Fair is kept; and he that will go to the City, and yet not go through this town, must needs go out of the world.
>
> John Bunyan

That the natural world should be recognised as real, and the channels between it and individual man kept open is to George Orwell no less than a moral necessity. The previous chapter sought to establish this fact and later chapters will show how organic such a belief is to his moral vision as a whole, and, in that context, will examine its seminal effect upon his art. But in these preliminary stages it is worth taking a little more time to draw attention to certain derivatives from Orwell's attachment to operating in nature which further endorse his self-proclaimed affinity with the Protestant tradition in that they describe a significant part of the psychology of Puritanism. The root is common since these so-called derivatives, as well as Orwell's particular attitude to nature, go back to the concept of the free individual with his personal contract with God, his 'rational, sceptical, experimental habit of mind', and his resignation to making his soul in the world around him. To identify these entirely characteristic elements in Orwell's response to life is, at the same time, to discover fresh links with his Protestant past, particularly that past as he himself saw it and conceived it as his literary heritage.

Here it had better be admitted that when we talk of the Protestant past or the Protestant consciousness what we usually have in mind has rather more to do with seventeenth-century Protestantism than sixteenth: so much of our notion of the term is a distillation of Milton, Bunyan and R. H. Tawney. In fact as this implies we tend to draw on the attributes of that more fundamental, less institutional sect, Puritanism. But this is, historically, unsurprising. It was part and product of the Protestant reformation and suceeded as Tawney showed in concentrating and crystallising the ethic in social and economic forms which ensured that its particular tenets would deeply – more deeply than any other, perhaps – imbue our cultural life. And it is no more than one would expect that the fundamentalist, latter-day Orwell should be attracted to the more rigorous side of the tradition.

Keeping in mind Tawney's seasonable admonition that 'ideas have a pedigree which, if realised, would often embarrass their exponents' we might, albeit riskily, catalogue the derivatives referred to above as follows: activism and a pragmatic commitment to the job nearest to hand, anti-intellectualism and an emphasis on will, anti-hedonism, a crusading sense of mission and an insistence on discipline, a belief in 'character' and the moral necessity of strenuous effort. All of these qualities are recognisably Orwellian and if Puritanism is much too complex a denomination for its psychology to be summarised in these terms, and the terms themselves too organic in their pedigree to allow themselves to be exclusively attached to Puritanism, nevertheless they do describe ingredients made familiar to us in Puritan writing of the last three centuries.

One of the many distinctions made of Puritanism holds that it is characterised by being 'rooted in a vast sense of dissatisfaction with mediocre and half-hearted endeavour' and what has been said about Orwell's belief in a saving discontent offers another example of his affinity. But for him, no less than for the earliest Protestant adherent, merely to keep alive this discontent was not enough. It embodied not a negative but a constructive reformist force, and its theatre was undoubtedly the natural world and the daily lives of men. Orwell's inability to accept any transcendent existence made such an emphasis inevitable but at the same time it was one which might be seen to derive from the tradition to which he affiliated himself. Writing of the Diggers' leader, Gerrard Winstanley, Professor Sabine notes that he was typical of his time and place in the Puritan revolution:

It is characteristic of Winstanley, and also of others who were most given to these [millenarian] expectations, that they looked for the literal and, so to speak, the physical realisation of the Kingdom of God on earth. It is a mere trick of self-seeking priests, he thought, to fob men off with hopes of a better life beyond the grave . . . instead of urging them to create the New Jerusalem here and now. Flesh judges it right that some should be poor and others rich and powerful, but in the light of equity and reason it is right that all should have freedom and subsistence.[1]

Though Orwell's pragmatism was not incorporated in any chiliastic vision (in the literal sense, anyway) he does not seem at all remote from his antecedents in a comment such as this:

To raise the standard of living of the whole world to that of Britain would not be a greater undertaking than the war we are now fighting. I don't claim, and I don't know who does, that that would solve anything in itself. It is merely that privation and brute labour have to be abolished before the real problems of humanity can be tackled. The major problem of our time is the decay of the belief in personal immortality, and it cannot be dealt with while the average human being is either drudging like an ox or shivering in fear of the secret police. How right the working classes are in their 'materialism'! How right they are to realise that the belly comes before the soul, not in the scale of values but in point of time![2]

Despite the edge his pragmatism takes from his disbelief in anything other than a terrestrial New Jerusalem it is quite clear that the divorce between the terrestrial and the heavenly is by no means complete. It is quite typical of him that he should see the loss of faith in personal immortality as the major problem of our time.

There is an instructive comparison to be made here with Kipling. He, too, retains a recognisably Puritan pragmatism, embedded as it is in all the other qualities just enumerated; but, while also seeking to improve the material lot of people, his break with the transcendental is far more complete. His is still a Puritan cosmos, without, however, any trace of God. In consequence, his perspective is exceptionally bleak: for him pragmatism and activity assume as their principal objective the preservation of self-consciousness. In the quotation which follows it is not because life is not long enough that one does not 'waste' it on metaphysical speculation: it is that to do so would be to render life (as self-consciousness) impossible:

> Naturally a man (in Town) grows to think that there is no one higher than himself, and that the Metropolitan Board of Works made everything. But, in India, where you really see humanity – raw, brown, naked humanity – with nothing between it and the blazing sky, and only the used-up, overhandled earth underfoot, the notion somehow dies away, and most folk come back to simpler theories. Life, in India, is not long enough to waste in proving that there is no one in particular at the head of affairs. For this reason. The Deputy is above the Assistant, the Commissioner above the Deputy, the Lieutenant-Governor above the Commissioner, and the Viceroy above all four, under the orders of the Secretary of State, who is responsible to the Empress. If the Empress be not responsible to her Maker – if there is no Maker for her to be responsible to – the entire system of Our administration must be wrong. Which is manifestly impossible.[3]

Work is a ritual, a moral cement; and as a character of his remarks elsewhere: 'All Ritual is fortifying. Ritual's a natural necessity for mankind. The more things are upset, the more they fly to it.'[*4]

Kipling in ostentatiously deriding the reality of any other problem in comparison with the physical does two things. He shows that there *is* another problem (which turns out to be that of establishing a coherent 'self'), and he clarifies the difference between his own remarkably unillusioned vision where the only reality is chaos, all else being artifice, and Orwell's where commitment to the physical world is a means to what is really a spiritual end. Yet in both passages there is an unacknowledged tension, underlined particularly in their closing sentences. Kipling's mannered nonchalance is intended to convey

---

* I discuss this and other aspects of Kipling in *The Wheel of Empire* (Macmillam 1967) pp. 64–113.

to us the impression of someone who has achieved easy control over the moral complexities of existence; when in fact he lives in terror lest the fragile structure he has so laboriously erected as a barricade against self-annihilating chaos should give way. Orwell in his praise of the working class's good sense is a little too defiant. There is, it seems to me, not just righteous fervour in his exhortation to go for the pie in the hand rather than the pie in the sky but suppressed anger against a pie-less empyrean and the burden which its emptiness entails.

On odd occasions this anger turns into near-defeatism and confidence in his moral purpose weakens. It is then that commitment becomes less to the doctrine of the free personality, and more to commitment. In the words of Dorothy Hare in *A Clergyman's Daughter*, 'if one gets on with the job that lies nearest to hand, the ultimate purpose of the job fades into insignificance'.[5] This is verging on Kipling's attitude that commitment is necessary so that identity can be appropriated from whatever it is that commitment has created. But in itself such a position could be seen as an historical development of the moral self-sufficiency to which the Puritan had laid claim in staking all upon his responsibility and capacity for making his own private contract with God – who, to Kipling at least, no longer exists. As Tawney put it:

> Those who seek God in isolation from their fellowmen, unless trebly armed for the perils of the quest, are apt to find, not God, but a devil, whose countenance bears an embarrassing resemblance to their own.[6]

The danger was very real for those who despised the world in which they made their souls, and who were by their faith deprived of much sense of an organic communion between themselves and their fellow men. Physical activity in the natural world was for such essential, not as a means of salvation but as a sign that God's grace had been bestowed:

> . . . what is rejected as a means is resumed as a consequence, and the Puritan flings himself into practical activities with the daemonic energy of one who, all doubts allayed, is conscious that he is a sealed and chosen vessel . . . Tempered by self-examination, self-discipline,

self-control, he is the practical ascetic, whose victories are won not in the cloister, but on the battlefield, in the counting-house, and in the market.[7]

Certainly Orwell could not be said to have despised the world in which he 'made his soul'; while action for him was *both* a means of salvation and proof that salvation had been accorded. Fundamentally, it was the executive act of the personal self, suitably fulfilled in that constitutional banging about among solid objects which made the world go round – or, at least, gave one the means of proving to one's own satisfaction that it did, thus vindicating the concept of the personal self. In such a process it was axiomatic that something like a moral sanction would be conferred upon the glorification of action and the man of action. Had Orwell accepted the likelihood of a Day of Doom instead of regretting its evaporation, his position could have been summed up by Bunyan:

> . . . at the day of doom, men shall be judged according to their fruits. It will not be said then, 'Did you believe?' but, 'Were you *doers*, or *talkers* only?' and accordingly shall they be judged.[8]

As it is, one recalls his appreciation of Kipling's Anglo-Indians who, if not sympathetic characters, 'were at any rate people who did things'.[9]

In fact, his admiration for the doer receives early and extravagant ventilation in *Burmese Days*. The eternal fourth-former in Orwell is describing through the medium of Flory the new arrival at Kyauktada:

> He was a youth of about twenty-five, lank but very straight, and manifestly a cavalry officer. He had one of those rabbit-like faces common among English soldiers, with pale blue eyes and a little triangle of fore-teeth visible between the lips; yet hard, fearless and even brutal in a careless fashion – a rabbit, perhaps, but a tough and martial rabbit. He sat his horse as though he were part of it, and he looked offensively young and fit.[10]

Here it is the military activist who exercises the appeal but Orwell's attraction to the principle is sufficient to lead to a variety of incarnations. The pleasure he took in seeing man as an industrious cog working in its allotted place in the great machine has been alluded to earlier; while in, for example, *The Road to Wigan Pier* we find activism to be of the staunch Puritan sort which associates strenuous effort in the practical world with the moral wholeness of the individual. In *Homage to Catalonia*, to take yet another case, the activist ethic is impressively assimilated to a subtle projection of man's place and role in the history of his culture; an ample fulfilment of Orwell's description of art as 'a registration, as it were, of man's attitude to the Universe at any given moment'.[11]

It is significant, in this connection, that the time he spent in Spain during the Civil War was one of the happiest of his life. The reasons are complex, and will be scrutinised more closely later, but it is true that in action there he found briefly the community he continually sought for, and in *Homage to Catalonia* he celebrates his involvement with, at times, an almost mystical ardour worthy of his distinguished predecessors in the tradition. 'It is action' said Richard Baxter the great Puritan preacher, 'that God is most served and honoured by';[12] and Orwell, as we shall see, is often found to be reaching *through* action to a state that is decidedly spiritual.

There are, however, elements of a very much cruder order. Far too intelligent and commonsensical to glorify war he is nevertheless capable of striking a note that would have been approved by Sir Garnet Wolseley himself:

> To survive you often have to fight, and to fight you have to dirty yourself. War is evil, and it is often the lesser evil. Those who take the sword perish by the sword, and those who don't take the sword perish by smelly diseases. The fact that such a platitude is worth writing down shows what the years of *rentier* capitalism have done to us.[13]

It is a passage which certainly recalls Kipling's condescension towards those who die 'decently' of zymotic diseases.

His admiration of the doer leads to some comical results when, for instance, he rather sheepishly indulges a tendency to swashbuckle. Writing to Cyril Connolly he cannot resist the last sentence: 'A pity you didn't come up to our position and see me when you were in Aragon. I would have enjoyed giving you tea in a dug-out'.[14] Also, it is hard to believe that this sentence to Rayner Heppenstall really originated in a desire to act as guinea-pig for a threatened generation: 'I am rather glad to have been hit by a bullet because I think it will happen to us all in the near future, and I am glad to know that it doesn't hurt to speak of.'[15] A sentence like 'But it was a handy little bomb to throw' doesn't quite convince us, and the brigand in this one is up-staged by the grammarian: 'If they had been good party-men they would, I suppose, have urged me to change sides, or even have pinioned me and taken away the bombs of which my pockets were full.'[16] He even succeeds in giving a modest harvesting operation on Jura the stature of the Normandy invasion: 'Thanks ever so for the tea – it came just at the right moment because this week the whole of the nearest village is being brought here in lorries to get in the field of corn in front of our house, and of course tea will have to flow like water while the job is on'.[17] The impression of such description is charming and threefold: primarily we see an Orwell who relished acting and activity; secondly, that he is not at heart a fierce anarchist – there is some other point of reference outside this which makes his talk of bombs a little incongruous: and, lastly, a man with a rather child-like appeal who doesn't always know how to orientate himself to the expectations of the adult world.

Despite this attraction towards an activist 'philosophy' he is too much of an artist himself not to sympathise with the dilemma the contemporary writer finds himself in vis-à-vis commitment. In his essay on Henry Miller he does not directly criticise him for the lack of any 'impulse to alter or control the process that he is undergoing' though it is equally obvious that he cannot share such an attitude:

> He has performed the essential Jonah act of allowing himself to be swallowed, remaining passive, *accepting*.
>
> It will be seen what this amounts to. It is a species of quietism, implying either complete unbelief or else a degree of belief amounting to mysticism. The attitude is 'Je m'en fous' or 'Though He slay me yet will I trust in Him', whichever way you look at it; for practical purposes both are identical, the moral in either case being 'Sit on your

bum'.[18]

For the creative writer in 1940, however, he accepts gloomily that there might be no alternative:

> . . . from now onwards the all-important fact for the creative writer is going to be that this is not a writer's world. That does not mean that he cannot help to bring the new society into being, but he can take no part in the process *as a writer*. For *as a writer* he is a liberal, and what is happening is the destruction of liberalism.[19]

To understand the writer's predicament is not, however, to excuse far less accept the circumstances that have made him what he is. 'Inside the Whale' is full of resentment at the apparent defeat of the active principle:

> . . . unquestionably our own age, at any rate in Western Europe, is less healthy and less hopeful than the age in which Whitman was writing. Unlike Whitman, we live in a *shrinking* world. The 'democratic vistas' have ended in barbed wire. There is less feeling of creation and growth, less and less emphasis on the cradle, endlessly rocking, more and more emphasis on the teapot endlessly stewing. To accept civilisation *as it is* practically means accepting decay. It has ceased to be a strenuous attitude and becomes a passive attitude – even 'decadent', if that word means anything.[20]

There was, in fact, never any likelihood of Orwell actually giving up the struggle whether as writer or simply as political being, though a fascination with the possibility of surrender is such an integral part of his nature that it provides the major tension in most of his works and culminates in the pessimistic vision of *Nineteen Eighty-Four* where submission is accepted as the only reality. Earlier his response is still that of a stern, over-simplifying Puritan. In his review of *The Rock Pool*, he takes Cyril Connolly severely in hand:

> The awful thraldom of money is upon everyone and there are only three immediately obvious escapes. One is religion, another is unending work, the third is the kind of sluttish antinomianism – lying in bed till four in the afternoon,

drinking Pernod – that Mr. Connolly seems to admire. The
third is certainly the worst, but in any case the essential evil
is to think in terms of *escape*.[21]

That this should be the 'essential evil' is characteristic: yet,
paradoxically, Orwell thought all the time of escape. Perhaps
one might suspect something of the kind from the intense
repugnance he frequently showed towards 'softness' and to
those who would '[rob] reality of its terrors by simply submitting to it'[22] a remark and an attitude very reminiscent of a
latter-day Puritan like Carlyle. To both he opposes a doctrine
of toughness and strenuous effort. 'Softness is repulsive' he
tells us in *The Road to Wigan Pier*[23] – sounding for a moment
dangerously like Milton's Satan – and all unbeknown, it is
creeping up on us in the guise of progress: 'The implied objective of "progress" is – not *exactly*, perhaps, the brain in the
bottle, but at any rate some frightful sub-human depth of softness and helplessness.'[24] Submissiveness and softness are the
lure of the Devil, and a familiar one at that. Here is Richard
Steele's version of sluttish antinomianism (from *The
Tradesman's Calling, being a Discourse concerning the Nature, Necessity, Choice etc. of a Calling in general, 1684*):

> The standing pool is prone to putrefaction; and it were
> better to beat down the body and to keep it in subjection by
> a laborious calling, than through luxury to become a
> castaway.[25]

Perhaps this Puritan prototype was a little more alive to the
fleshly possibilities of sloth; if so it would suggest that though
his and Orwell's quarrel with the body took different forms
the source might have been common to both. Matthew Henry
gets more succinctly and sharply to the point with his remark
that 'Those that are prodigal of their time despise their own
souls.' Zwingli himself appears to have had a suspicion not
unlike Orwell's that strenuous effort was a thing of the past:

> With labour will no man now support himself . . . And yet
> labour is a thing so good and godlike that makes the body
> hale and strong and cures the sicknesses produced by idle-
> ness . . . In the things of this life, the labourer is most like to
> God.[26]

Admit ignoble ease and peaceful sloth and the soul is indeed at risk, for effort and activity which are the proof of salvation (of, in Orwell's case, the validity of the personal self) and its means, will be neutralised. Go beyond the minimum alleviation of hardship necessary to an ascetic human dignity, so Orwell maintains, and the spiritual dynamic which is generated in the individual's direct confrontation with his world and embodied in the notion of the personal self, disappears. The passion with which he customarily chastises the slothful and the 'luxurious' declares itself all too clearly in *The Lion and the Unicorn: Socialism and the English Genius*. After full allowance has been made for its war-time context, its strident championship of the activist ideal betrays the unacknowledged and irrational depth of partisanship which the subject rouses in the author:

> During the past twenty years the negative, *fainéant* outlook which has been fashionable among English left-wingers, the sniggering of the intellectuals at patriotism and physical courage, the persistent effort to chip away English morale and spread a hedonistic, what-do-I-get-out-of-it attitude to life, has done nothing but harm. It would have been harmful even if we had been living in the squashy League of Nations universe that these people imagined. In an age of Fuehrers and bombing planes it was a disaster. However little we may like it, toughness is the price of survival. A nation trained to think hedonistically cannot survive amid peoples who work like slaves and breed like rabbits, and whose chief national industry is war.[27]

In a review of some of Jack London's short stories Orwell asserts that 'London could foresee Fascism because he had a Fascist streak himself.'[28] One is tempted to draw the same inference about Orwell when one comes across this in an earlier article called 'Prophecies of Fascism':

> . . . one can see [by comparing *The Iron Heel* with *The Sleeper Awakes*] both London's limitations and also the advantage he enjoyed in not being, like Wells, a fully civilised man . . . because of his own streak of savagery London could grasp something that Wells apparently could not, and this is that hedonistic societies do not endure.[29]

Reviewing *Mein Kampf* Orwell is extremely honest in making clear the fascination evoked by the image which he insists is Hitler's own view of himself. (It is worth noticing how Hitler's given view shades into Orwell's own.)

> He is the martyr, the victim, Prometheus chained to the rock, the self-sacrificing hero who fights single-handed against impossible odds . . . One feels, as with Napoleon, that he is fighting against destiny, that he *can't* win, and yet that he somehow deserves to. The attraction of such a pose is of course enormous . . .
>
> Also he has grasped the falsity of the hedonistic attitude to life. Nearly all western thought since the last war, certainly all 'progressive' thought, has assumed tacitly that human beings desire nothing beyond ease, security and avoidance of pain. In such a view of life there is no room, for instance, for patriotism and the military values. Hitler, because in his own joyless mind he feels it with exceptional strength, knows that human beings *don't* only want comfort, safety, short working-hours, hygiene, birth-control and, in general, common-sense; they also, at least intermittently, want struggle and self-sacrifice, not to mention drums, flags and loyalty-parades. However they may be as economic theories, Fascism and Nazism are psychologically far sounder than any hedonistic conception of life.[30]

As Milton's Satan, that archetype of muscular, anti-intellectual activism puts it: '. . . to be weak is miserable/Doing or suffering'. And there are moments in his denunciation of softness when Orwell seems to share the conviction and even to project the implications alarmingly:

> I . . . have a vague feeling that in our century there is some sort of inter-connection between the quality of thought and culture in a country and the *size* of the country.[31]

Vague or not it is a doctrine of *lebensraum* and when this is linked to a tendency to project an image of Hitler akin to Shelley's view of the Satan of *Paradise Lost* one may justifiably wonder if the devil's party is about to get a new fellow-traveller.

With his instinctive attraction to physical activism, his dedi-
cation to a basic contact with the natural world, and his admiration for the doer, it was fairly inevitable that Orwell should
find an ideal type in working-class man. Other factors in this
relationship, such as the reason for his sentimentalising him,
will emerge later, but if we look for a moment now at *The Road
to Wigan Pier* we can see not just his concern with the physical
but the contrast he draws between it and the intellectual life.
One quotation will be sufficient to show his fascination with
the working-class doer: the Lawrentian-in-spite-of-himself
(the informative parenthesis being typically Orwellian)
description of the miners at work.

> . . . the fillers look and work as though they were made of
> iron. They really do look like iron – hammered iron statues
> – under the smooth coat of coal dust which clings to them
> from head to foot. It is only when you see miners down the
> mine and naked that you realise what splendid men they
> are. Most of them are small (big men are at a disadvantage
> in that job) but nearly all of them have the most noble
> bodies; wide shoulders tapering to slender supple waists,
> and small pronounced buttocks and sinewy thighs, with not
> an ounce of waste flesh anywhere. In the hotter mines they
> wear only a pair of thin drawers, clogs, and knee-pads, in
> the hottest mines of all, only the clogs and knee-pads. You
> can hardly tell by the look of them whether they are young
> or old. They may be any age up to sixty or even sixty-five,
> but when they are black and naked they all look alike. No
> one could do their work who had not a young man's body,
> and a figure fit for a guardsman at that; just a few pounds of
> extra flesh on the waist-line, and the constant bending
> would be impossible. You can never forget that spectacle
> once you have seen it – the line of bowed, kneeling figures,
> sooty black all over, driving their huge shovels under the
> coal with stupendous force and speed.[32]

It is characteristic of later Puritan writers that to varying
degrees they express admiration for the working man, a
regard – sometimes reluctant – for the aristocrat, and a contempt for the middle class in which the movement had had its
origins and most powerful support. Also characteristic is a

tendency to asperse the meditative life in comparison with the more robust virtues of the labourer 'most like to God'. This goes with a profound belief in 'character': Tawney, describing how Calvinism stood for a new scale of moral values and a new ideal of social conduct, suggested that its practical message might be said to be '*La carrière ouverte* – not *aux talents*, but *au caractère*'[33]

Orwell again shows his Protestant fundamentalism in his attitude to the education of the working-class, prompting us to recall, amongst other things, that in his essay on Kipling he had thoroughly approved the prescriptive wisdom of the latter's 'Gods of the Copy-book Headings'. The working-class boy, at least, is ready to accept Experience as his teacher and is evidently all the healthier for it:

> Of course I know that there is not one working-class boy in a thousand who does not pine for the day when he will leave school. He wants to be doing real work, not wasting his time on ridiculous rubbish like history and geography. To the working class, the notion of staying at school till you are nearly grown-up seems merely contemptible and unmanly. The idea of a great big boy of eighteen, who ought to be bringing a pound a week home to his parents, going to school in a ridiculous uniform and even being caned for not doing his lessons! Just fancy a working-class boy of eighteen allowing himself to be caned! He is a man when the other is still a baby. Ernest Pontifex, in Samuel Butler's *Way of all Flesh*, after he had had a few glimpses of real life, looked back on his public school and university education and found it a 'sickly, debilitating debauch'. There is much in middle-class life that looks sickly and debilitating when you see it from a working-class angle.[34]

Orwell is studiously careful not to identify himself with the view, speaking in the voice of the working class. But where, if we accept this, do Ernest Pontifex and his creator Samuel Butler – emphatically not of the working class – come in? And with what purpose?

Gerrard Winstanley in his pamphlet 'The New Law of Righteousness' (1649) vigorously attacked 'those learned University men that despise the unlearned' describing them in a memorable phrase as 'pricks of the thornbush, not branches of the vine'.[35] Orwell – to whom the metaphor would surely have been congenial – carries the argument to greater extremes, transposing the contempt to the other side, and at the same time making it quite clear that the working man who allowed himself to be seduced from his class by the false prophecies of a higher education lost all virtue. Consequently, his ideal community comes to resemble a closed monastic system tightly organised round the twin virtues of Work and Decency. The essential conservatism of the Puritan (and, in the penultimate sentence, a surprising political naiveté) comes through strongly here:

> . . . the working-class intelligentsia is sharply divisible into two different types. There is the type who remains working class – who goes on working as a mechanic or a dock-labourer or whatever it may be and does not bother to change his working-class accent and habits, but who 'improves his mind' in his spare time and works for the I.L.P. or the Communist Party; and there is the type who does alter his way of life, at least externally, and who by means of State Scholarships succeeds in climbing into the middle class. The first is one of the finest types of man we have. I can think of some I have met whom not even the most hidebound Tory could help liking and admiring. The other type, with exceptions – D. H. Lawrence, for example – is less admirable.

The contempt for those found 'climbing into' another class is unmistakable:

> The 'clever' boy of a working-class family, the sort of boy who wins scholarships, and is obviously not fitted for a life of manual labour, may find other ways of rising into the class above – a slightly different type, for instance, rises via Labour Party politics – but the literary way is by far the most usual. Literary London now teems with young men who are of proletarian origin and have been educated by means of scholarships. Many of them are very disagreeable people, quite unrepresentative of their class. . . .[36]

But Orwell's anti-intellectualism is not simply a negative

affair. Intellectuals and the intelligentsia, as has been suggested, challenged his basic creed both morally and politically. Reviewing *The Edge of the Abyss* he agrees with Noyes that 'the intelligentsia are more infected by totalitarian ideas than the common people',[37] and in '*The Lion and the Unicorn*' he chastises their fondness for 'balancing democracy against totalitarianism and 'proving' that one is as bad as the other.'[38] Dismayed at the confusion and danger such attitudes could create, Orwell put his faith in the common-sense empiricism of the 'ordinary' English citizenry and particularly of the working-class: but if this bulwark were breached, those sleight-of-hand theorisers would dree their weird, (and we might note again the debt expressed to the Reformation):

> Whoever tries to undermine their faith in Democracy, to chip away the moral code they derive from the Protestant centuries and the French Revolution, is not preparing power for himself, though he may be preparing it for Hitler . . .[39]

Morally the intellectual fifth-column, with their clever metaphysics, had the power to subvert men from their allegiance to the natural world and natural laws; a power that is recognised explicitly when Orwell admits to having 'a perfect horror of a dictatorship of theorists'.[40] Consequently it is never enough for him just to demonstrate their political unreliability or their passive indifference to reform: they have to be shown as deficient in that tough moral fibre necessary for the continuous conflict which was a condition of existence for those who based their creed on the reformist doctrine of personal responsibility and freedom of individual conscience.

So the miners slaving away in naked majesty are sacrificing themselves to sustain the wicked, the dishonest, the idle, and that Sporus of contemporary society, the dilettante intellectual:

> In order that Hitler may march the goose step, that the Pope may denounce Bolshevism, that the cricket crowds may assemble at Lords, that the Nancy poets may scratch one another's backs, coal has got to be forthcoming.[41]

Intellectuals, it seems are effete degenerates, embarrassingly deficient in manliness, thoroughly deserving such contemptuous labels as the 'Pansy Left' or the 'boiled rabbits of the left'. (Kipling's 'Recessional' is apparently something of a touchstone; 'Lesser breeds without the Law' being 'always good for a snigger in pansy-left circles'.[42]) Conscientious objectors, initially at any rate, merited special castigation and they got plenty in Orwell's reply to Alex Comfort's jibes from the pacifist side at the 'buffer, fool and patrioteer':

> I wrote in nineteen-forty that at need
> I'd fight to keep the Nazis out of Britain;
> And Christ! how shocked the pinks were . . . .
> . . . .
> Yet where's the pink that would have thought it odd of me
> To write a shelf of books in praise of sodomy?[43]

Describing an incident in Burma he strikes a similar note even more distastefully:

> I remember once when I was inspecting a police station, an American missionary whom I knew fairly well came in for some purpose or other. Like most Nonconformist missionaries he was a complete ass but quite a good fellow. One of my native sub-inspectors was bullying a suspect (I described this scene in *Burmese Days*). The American watched it, and then turning to me said thoughtfully, 'I wouldn't care to have your job'. It made me horribly ashamed. So *that* was the kind of job I had! Even an ass of an American missionary, a teetotal cock-virgin from the Middle West, had the right to look down on me and pity me![44]

The bluff, hearty attitude of the colonial 'doer' towards the interfering missionary is a commonplace of the literature of Empire, and the source of it is always the same: exasperation at having practical necessities obscured and frustrated by those who worked to other priorities. For Orwell, of course, it is complicated by the guilt he feels. Still, for him to be quite so contemptuous is a little surprising and shows just how much of an investment he had in the activist ideal. It certainly endows a comment he makes in *The Road to Wigan Pier* with some agreeable irony:

> This nonsense about the superior energy of the English (actually the laziest people in Europe) has been current for at least a hundred years. 'Better is it for us', writes a Quarterly Reviewer of 1827, 'to be condemned to labour for our country's good than to luxuriate amid olives, vines, and vices.' 'Olives, vines, and vices' sums up the normal English attitude towards the Latin races.[45]

There is, perhaps, another element in Orwell's anti-intellectualism. His impatience with the mode is, in many ways that of the man so sure in his revealed faith that abstract intellectual analyses and analysts by being what they are miss the point. It is a credal mistrust of metaphysics which was characteristic of Luther himself, and as J.S. Whale suggests in *The Protestant Tradition*, well summed-up in Pascal's phrase 'Dieu . . . non des philosophes et des savants'. Like so many of his precursors Orwell had no confidence in the intellectual's ability to discover the answers to problems of living — quite the contrary. Again Gerrard Winstanley could have stood as mentor for this sort of self-sufficiency:

> Goe read all the books in your Universitie, that tels you what hath been formerly, and though you can make speeches of a day long from those readings yet you shall have no peace, but your hearts still shal be a barren wildernesse, and encrease in sorrow till your eyes return into your selves, and the spirit come from on high to make you read in your own book your heart.[46]

Perhaps too from the same impatience and self-sufficiency comes the authoritarian element in Orwell's temper.

*　*　*

'One thing I promise you Martin,' says Staupitz to Luther in John Osborne's play, 'You'll never be a spectator. You'll always take part.' So it was for Orwell, motivated by a dynamic which he regarded as characteristically Protestant. If truth and integrity — even soul — depend on man having a personal and empirical relationship to his moral universe, then the individual's voice is of significance. Participation will already be a condition of his moral existence and with the enhanced sense of responsibility the new freedom brings, will have its field of operation steadily increased. It will certainly not be confined to spiritual concerns as the Peasant's War all too clearly demonstrated to Luther. Reformism, the desire, the need and, after Luther the *obligation* to question, repudiate and assert will stop only where conscience allows it to. The zeal for reform as Professor Woodhouse has pointed out is 'one of the most constant and indisputable notes of Puritanism' and he quotes in *Puritanism and Liberty* from one of Thomas Case's sermons:

> Reform the universities . . . Reform the cities . . . the countries . . . the sabbath, . . . the ordinances, the worship of God . . . *Every plant which my heavenly Father hath not planted shall be rooted up.*[47]

The Reformation, in giving moral sanction and moral structure to the vast energy of Renaissance individualism, and in removing the necessity for mediation was quite deliberately seeking a reintegration of conscience, and therefore religion, with daily life. Only in contact with the material world could full proof be given of man's capacity for personal responsibility, and indeed for salvation. Adam and Eve 'with wandering steps and slow' show their reluctance to leave the richness and security of Eden for the bleak outer world full of snares and pitfalls, but only in doing so can they and their descendants prove God's mercy justified.

How well Orwell fits into the Protestant or, more accurately, Puritan tradition the foregoing pages have attempted to show. There is certainly a missionary's ardour in his determination to communicate his belief (and to convert others to it) that salvation lay through observance of the natural laws and empirical contact with the material world. Obviously there could never be any case of his being a spectator. He has a doctrine to preach, which, in its emphasis on the individual's right to a direct, personal interpretation of experience and its insistence on alerting people to the fundamental importance of 'operating in nature', has a substantial likeness to its Puritan original. Even more than the latter it stresses the practical, and enjoins activist participation as both an earnest of faith and the means of creating a better society. Like the earlier Puritan described by Tawney his task was 'at once to discipline his individual life and to create a sanctified society.' The adjective is not really too strong applied to Orwell. From what has been said so far, it is clear that his search for betterment extends well beyond material care, as he struggles to identify and sustain a morality in the face of totalitarian encroachment. His honest, empirical pursuit of this goal is the one 'sanctified' by Milton in *Areopagitica*:

> To be still searching what we know not by what we know, still closing up truth to truth as we find it . . . this is the golden rule in theology as well as in arithmetic. . . .[48]

Philip Rieff in his extremely interesting essay 'George Orwell and the post-Liberal Imagination' maintains that the basis of action for Orwell was simply the need 'to meet the demands of the day', which he rightly classifies as 'an ethic of action – for the morally exhausted.' But while it might be difficult to exonerate Kipling – writing out of the same Puritan background and also attaching much importance to action – from such a charge, with Orwell it is a different matter. Significantly Rieff draws his principal evidence for the remark from one source. *A Clergyman's Daughter.* Referring to Dorothy's resolution to settle simply for the job that lies nearest to hand, he goes on:

> In the liberal theory, only the exhaustion of activity can counter the exhaustion of morality. 'The glue had liquefied. The problem of faith and no faith had vanished utterly from her mind. It was beginning to get dark, but, too busy to stop and light the lamp, she worked on, pasting strip after strip into place, with absorbed, with pious concentration, in the penetrating smell of the glue-pot'. These are the final sentences of *A Clergyman's Daughter*. Orwell's answer for Dorothy is his own. The only available liberal substitute for faith was the action of gluing together what has fallen into pieces. Glue replaces Christian love as the sign of unity in the religion of the exhausted. One has to be completely outside religious experience to conceive of religion as most basically a mode of social cohesion. And, indeed, from

Feuerbach to Durkheim, the liberals had known faith was nothing except its function as glue. Unity was the needful thing. (Whether it was called caritas or phallus worship was only an accidental distinction.) It was plain to Orwell, in his intellectual integrity, that the liberal-Christian civilization was irrevocably exhausted, but it was necessary to act as if it were not.[49]

This is completely wide of the mark. For one thing there is an ambiguity in Dorothy's attitude which suggests that she may not in fact be morally exhausted: '*pious*' concentration means something more than simply giving all one's attention to the job in hand. Of much greater importance however is it to challenge the remark that Orwell's answer for Dorothy is his own. It may be so in *The Clergyman's Daughter*, though even there one can by no means be sure. It certainly is not Orwell's own view as a whole: no other book offers this message and it is tempting to speculate that this was at least part of the reason why Orwell sought to suppress the book. It is simply not true that elsewhere he asserts religion as basically a mode of social cohesion with action consequently downgraded to an antidote for doubt, as Tennyson put it, or a mere psychological expedient for holding the self together. If he had done so he would have been much more Kiplingesque than he is and infinitely more negative. It is, too, a quite inadequate summary of his attitude to the liberal-Christian tradition to say that to him it was irrevocably exhausted though one had to act as if it were not. This is to make him live in a Conradian world of deliberately created illusions which does not square with the evidence. It is true that on various occasions he reached the gloomy conclusion that the tradition was on its very last legs, more than once, even, writing its obituary; but always he returned to fight the battle. Certainly he thought the liberal-Christian culture menaced and possibly heading for extinction, but he could conceive of no other premise for living and so prepared himself to defend it to the last. At other times still, his defence is so spirited and ebullient that his doubts seem to have vanished. Until his last book he is capable of laying his emphasis on any of these different projections.

Of course there were occasions when in the best Puritan

tradition confidence in his purpose and in his capacity to save the individual waned and we see him soldiering on simply through an exertion of will. But for the rest he is as purposeful as was the Daniel of the revivalist hymn. In 'Why I write' he tabulates the motives, as he sees them, 'for writing prose':

1. Sheer egoism. Desire to seem clever, to be talked about, to be remembered after death. . . . The great mass of human beings are not acutely selfish. After the age of about thirty they abandon individual ambition – in many cases, indeed, they almost abandon the sense of being individuals at all – and live chiefly for others or are simply smothered under drudgery. But there is also the minority of gifted wilful people who are determined to live their own lives to the end, and writers belong in this class. . . .

2. Aesthetic enthusiasm. Perception of beauty in the external world, or, on the other hand, in words and their right arrangement. . . .

3. Historical impulse. Desire to see things as they are, to find out true facts and store them up for posterity.

4. Political purpose – using the word 'political' in the widest possible sense. Desire to push the world in a certain direction, to alter other people's idea of the kind of society that they should strive after.[50]

Had Orwell carefully thought out a manifesto which would have proclaimed him to be a writer entirely within the Protestant tradition he could hardly have hit on anything more convincing than this brief adumbration.

But if what has been said so far were the sum of the effects of this tradition upon him and his writing, it would not – apart from the specificity, consistency and awareness with which the tradition is espoused – do much more than identify Orwell's provenance. It would not show how some of the most basic tensions of the Protestant response are not only there in Orwell but are an organic, indeed fundamental, part of his creative vision. To pursue this further, and to explain something of the real nature of that vision and its significance for his art, it is necessary to look at his relation to the darker

obverse of the more assertively self-sufficient side of Protestant
individualism.

4 The Frontier of Tragic Conscience

Locus noster in quo nos cum Deo, sponsus cum sponsa, habitare debet . . . est conscientia*

Martin Luther

Wealth addeth many friends: But the poor is separated from his friends.

Proverbs xix,4.

I dreamed, and behold I saw a man clothed with rags, standing in a certain place, with his face from his own house, a book in his hand and a great burden upon his back.

John Bunyan

In *Young Man Luther* Erik Erikson describes the mediaeval church as systematically and terroristically exploiting man's proclivity for a negative conscience. Latin Christianity in Luther's youth, he writes in explanation,

> tended to promise freedom from the body at the price of the absolute power of a negative external conscience: negative in that it was based on a sense of sin, and external in that it was defined and refined by a punitive agency which alone was aware of the rationale of morality and the consequences of disobedience.[1]

Luther, Erikson believes, was made for a job on the 'unconquered frontier of tragic conscience'. His special *locus* in other words, which he accepted for his life's work, is where the self 'can either live in wedded harmony with a positive conscience or is estranged from a negative one'. But Luther had not created the job; it having originated in

---

* Conscience is that inner ground where we and God have to learn to live with each other as man and wife.

the hypertrophy of the negative conscience inherent in our whole Judaeo-Christian heritage in which, as Luther put it: 'Christ becomes more formidable a tyrant and a judge than was Moses'. But the negative conscience can become hyper-trophied only when man hungers for his identity.[2]

The Reformation did nothing to ease man's proclivity for a negative conscience: to the contrary. Responsibility for estab-lishing a moral identity was now his alone since there no longer existed an intercessionary Church to provide him with a vicarious being. So if a vigorous and creative individualism was given impetus and spiritual sanction, the hunger for iden-tity was greater and more difficult to assuage, while loneliness and the sense of abandonment grew in its shadow. The dia-logue between Cajetan and Luther in John Osborne's play *Luther* compasses the development well and succinctly; Caje-tan predicting the deracination that will follow and Luther offering no comfort but his stark appeal to effort and duty:

Cajetan: Don't you see what could happen out of all this? Men could be cast out and left to themselves forever, helpless and frightened!
Martin: Your eminence, forgive me. I'm tired after my journey – I think I might faint soon –
Cajetan: That's what would become of them without their Mother Church – with all its imperfections, Peter's rock, without it they'd be helpless and unprotected. Allow them their sins, their petty indulgences, my son, they're unimportant to the comfort we receive –
Martin: (somewhat hysterical) Comfort! It doesn't concern me!
Cajetan: We live in thick darkness, and it grows thicker. How will men find God if they are left to themselves each man abandoned and only known to himself?
Martin: They'll have to try.[3]

To 'try' under the new dispensation, however, meant to be brought ever closer to the source of responsibility for weakness and failure: to one's self. If Luther had put Christ back where he belonged in each man's heart, or more specifically in each man's restless, dissatisfied conscience – he had indeed become a harsher judge than Moses, disclosing in the process that the obverse to the Reformers' self-confidence and optimism was an exaggerated sense of man's worthlessness, and an acute vulnerability to a crushing sense of guilt and sin which each man was seen to bear as his personal, inescapable burden.

Thus the Protestant becomes if anything more liable to the negative conscience and if it is the conspicuous example of Bunyan which springs most immediately to mind, the character taking shape here will suggest another.

In Orwell it is unquestionably the negative conscience which predominates; the obverse of his fierce individualism being an almost obsessive preoccupation with guilt and sin. A buoyant, confident sense of self readily yields to one which seems to exist only to make audible the voice of wrath. So strong is the negative conscience in him and so persistent is his search for absolution and moral identity that he turns back to that punitive agency 'which alone was aware of the rationale of morality and the consequences of disobedience', and seeks the wedded harmony of the positive conscience in the arms of the monopolists of salvation.

Down and Out in Paris and London is supposed to be about poverty and the book is duly furnished with an appropriate epigraph from Chaucer:

'O scathful harm, condition of poverte.'

Very early on in the Paris section we are told that the book will not dwell on the private lives of the quarter's inhabitants, considering them only in so far as these comment on the theme:

> I am trying to describe the people in our quarter, not for the mere curiosity, but because they are all part of the story. Poverty is what I am writing about, and I had my first contact with poverty in this slum. The slum, with its dirt and its queer lives, was first an object-lesson in poverty, and then the background of my own experiences.[4]

But from the start we are conscious of an ambiguity in his attitude to his chosen subject. The title itself alerts us: after all, it takes a man of some substance to be poor on *both* sides

of the Channel. Whiffs of its antecedents in Victorian travel
literature *On Horseback Through Asia Minor. A Pilgrimage to Nejd* –
come across to us sharpened perhaps by the parody in recent
titles like Eric Newby's *A Short Walk in the Hindu Kush.*

In fact, the Paris section of *Down and Out in Paris and London* is
about as much a description of poverty as *Europe on Five Dol-
lars a Day.* Orwell's ability to look upon his slum as an *object-
lesson* in poverty is symptomatic of his detachment from the
reality of poverty as a human affliction, calling in question his
sympathy for the condition and the real nature of his interest
in the subject. For much of the first part this interest would
seem to be merely that of the literary slummer whose best suit
can always in the last instance be redeemed. But this is by no
means the whole story and as the book progresses it becomes
less and less of the story. The condition of poverty has a deep
but highly personal significance for Orwell; of a sort, indeed,
which would suggest that the book's antecedents go back
beyond the world of Victorian globe-trotters to the wayfarers
of John Bunyan's rather different universe.

Life in the rue de Coq d'Or is as satisfyingly picturesque as
the street-name itself. Madame Monce shouts '*Salope! Salope!*
How many times have I told you not to squash bugs on the
wallpaper': Charlie tells a thrilling tale of unspeakable *fin de
siècle* vice in order that we should be shown 'what diverse
characters could be found flourishing in the Coq d'Or quarter': while Boris, the archetypal Russian *émigré*, accepts his
new station with all the courage and resourcefulness one
expects from an ex-captain in the Second Siberian Rifles
whose mistresses indulge themselves in baroque Caucasian
letter-writing to their 'Little Cherished Wolf'. There are
filthy attics with bug-ridden beds, consumptives, criminals,
grasping pawnbrokers: in fact it is difficult to think of anything left out of the Bohemian scene.

But it remains, of course, totally external, and the manner
of its telling self-consciously literary. In the last analysis it is
de Maupassant and not poverty that breathes through the
elaborately laconic vignettes and the vivid, superficial drama.
(And when it's not de Maupassant it's Somerset Maugham,
Zola, Conrad, Kipling or Oscar Wilde.) The most memorable
description is not really about poverty at all: it is of the

excitement, the bustle and the involvement in being a very humble member of the regiment of auxiliaries whose job it is to keep a great hotel running.

Despite one's awareness of all this, Orwell's candour about his detachment comes as something of a shock. It is, of course, all of a piece with the tone of the first part that he should in the midst of his harrowing circumstances be morally and financially capable of the bald statement:

> After ten days I managed to find a free quarter of an hour, and wrote to my friend B. in London asking him if he could get me a job of some sort – anything, so long as it allowed more than five hours sleep. I was simply not equal to going on with a seventeen hour day . . .
>
> . . . B. sent me a fiver to pay my passage and get my clothes out of the pawn, and as soon as the money arrived I gave one day's notice and left the restaurant.[5]

The casual way in which he extricates himself from his 'condition of poverte' cannot fail to damage the credibility of his claim to talk of poverty from the experienced inside – or to expose the superficiality of his relationship with the other citizens of the Coq d'Or. But this is compounded by another act, referred to earlier, that comes near to appalling us with its moral insensitivity:

> Then I washed my teeth for the first time in a fortnight, bathed and had my hair cut, and got my clothes out of pawn. I had two glorious days of loafing. I even went in my best suit to the Auberge, leant against the bar and spent five francs on a bottle of English beer. It is a curious sensation, being a customer where you have been a slave's slave.[6]

There is no saving embarrassment here, and certainly no pause to reflect on the offensiveness of his behaviour to those who could not wave a wand and appear transfigured, but were, for all their admirable qualities, condemned forever to be slaves' slaves. Unpalatable though it is, this is characteristically Orwellian. Like his Puritan predecessors he appears always to have a point to move to outside the immediate sphere of reference: always at the heart of his commitment there is a seed of inviolable self-sufficiency, a small area preserved for private contract. This was not basically a willed position – indeed it was a given quantity with its source in that tradition from which he drew his moral nourishment – but it was inevitable that it should set a barrier between him and those amongst whom he had to live. He tried hard to surmount that barrier yet there seems always to remain an element of equivocation. We could say of him, as Barbara Everett has said of W. H. Auden, that he sought a milieu in which his own individual experience could retain its separate existence and yet be domiciled within the experience of others. But it would not be the whole truth, for Orwell was too uncompromising for this to be an entirely satisfactory redaction. On one side of the barrier was a lonely individualism which gave him his moral being and on the other was a surrender to absolutism which would take it away. In this we have an outline of the major tension in Orwell's moral and artistic vision: and we will only begin to understand him when we recognise that the different sides of the barrier had an all but equal fascination.

Going down and out meant crossing a barrier and if we are to learn more of the moral significance of the process it is necessary to take a look at the role Orwell is imposing on the concept of poverty. It is noticeable for instance that he dwells a considerable time on the equation of poverty and persecution:

> You go to the baker's to buy a pound of bread, and you wait while the girl cuts a pound for another customer. She is clumsy, and cuts more than a pound. 'Pardon, Monsieur', she says, 'I suppose you don't mind paying two sous extra?' Bread is a franc a pound, and you have exactly a franc. When you think that you too might be asked to pay two sous extra, and would have to confess that you could not, you bolt in panic. It is hours before you dare venture into a baker's shop again.
> You go to the greengrocer's to spend a franc on a kilogram of potatoes. But one of the pieces that make up the franc is a Belgian piece, and the shopman refuses it. You slink out of

the shop, and can never go there again.

You have strayed into a respectable quarter, and you see a prosperous friend coming. To avoid him you dodge into the nearest café. Once in the café you must buy something, so you spend your last fifty centimes on a glass of black coffee with a dead fly in it. One could multiply these disasters by the hundred. They are part of the process of being hard up.[7]

That dead fly by itself proves Orwell's dogged determination to be victimised.

Clearly the persecution that poverty exposes one to registers unusually strongly on Orwell. Indeed, from the last quotation his sensitivity and vulnerability are sufficiently pronounced to encourage the impression that there is something pleasurable in the role of victim. It is by no means an isolated instance: the same response is in evidence throughout this and other works. Occasionally it has a gauche artlessness about it which, if anything, renders it more conspicuous. Going to work in the hotel, Orwell – and here a separate persona is being created, author and character are no longer coterminous – is led thrillingly down into subterranean depths beneath the hotel ('He led me down a winding staircase into a narrow passage, deep underground, and so low that I had to stoop in places. It was stiflingly hot and very dark . . .'). The *chef du personnel* takes him to

a tiny underground den – a cellar below a cellar, as it were – where there were a sink and some gas ovens. It was too low for me to stand quite upright, and the temperature was perhaps 110° Fahrenheit.

There he meets his superior:

'English, eh?' he said 'Well, I'm in charge here. If you work well' – he made the motion of up-ending a bottle and sucked noisily. 'If you don't' – he gave the doorpost several vigorous kicks. 'To me, twisting your neck would be no more than spitting on the floor. And if there's any trouble, they'll believe me, not you. So be careful.'

After this I set to work rather hurriedly.[8]

All that we can say to this is – goodness! Yet despite the

Boy's Own quality of the account there is enough substance to suggest that when Orwell, or 'Orwell', went to the dogs he was doing something more than exorcising his embarrassing bourgeois inheritance.

He is, in fact, quite explicit about 'another feeling that is a great consolation in poverty':

> It is a feeling of relief, almost of pleasure, at knowing yourself at last genuinely down and out. You have talked so often of going to the dogs – and, well, here are the dogs, and you have reached them, and you can stand it. It takes off a lot of anxiety.[9]

The complexity of his attitude to poverty can quite clearly be seen here in this mixture of fear, fascination, and relief. Something very much more than an objective description of the condition of poverty is involved. The fear of falling has been faced and overcome. Rock-bottom has at last been reached, and it brings not just relief but pleasure: a sense of liberation, perhaps; of freedom from the responsibility of having to struggle, to soldier on in the face of all the temptations and against all the odds. The succinct terseness of the very Orwellian last sentence – 'It takes off a lot of anxiety' – makes its face-value less rather than more scrutable, while 'anxiety', so carefully inexplicit in its context, and with just so much more pressure behind it than might be thought warranted in the circumstances hints at the larger dimension of his concern. Specifically we are told of his discovery of another 'great redeeming feature of poverty' in the fact that 'it annihilates the future'.[10] 'Annihilate' is a fairly extreme term but it is frequently used by Orwell (so are alternatives like 'wipe out' and 'erase'), indicating the hold exercised over him by the concept it embodies: there may be fear in it but there is as much attraction.

The second part of *Down and Out in Paris and London*, though also about poverty, is much less mannered and self-conscious and much less reticent. In the first part the narrator occasionally hints at a highly interesting and very personal involvement and at other times blandly affects the role of a mere projectionist of *cinéma vérité* but in fact he fulfills neither promise. It is quite different when Orwell comes to talk of his life with the tramps: here his account provides plenty of evidence of a real moral presence. And the explanation is not just that the picturesque degradation of the Coq d'Or is non-convertible; there is a significant shift in emphasis which comes about with the growth of a distinct persona exhibiting a highly particular relationship to the condition and people described as the book's subject.

In fact, while the picture the London section gives of the lot of tramps is vivid and memorable, it is the actions and reactions of the persona which give a superior quality and significance to the book. Through its agency there develops a moral dimension little more than hinted at in the earlier half. Orwell allows this character's highly personal reaction to poverty to develop freely following its own apparently intrinsic perspective, and the result is that we in turn learn more about him and it, and much more about the author's moral vision.

It is easy to underestimate the art which allows such access. Repeatedly in the second half we find the writing showing an attention to structure and balance which permits image and theme to expand until they enter a different world from that of the documentary. There is an example of this in the description of Orwell undergoing his transformation into a tramp, which is also a mutation of Orwell into 'Orwell'. He goes to a rag-shop in Lambeth to acquire clothes more suitable to his purpose. The shopman selects some of the filthiest and throws them over the counter in exchange for what Orwell is wearing:

> 'What about the money?' I said hoping for a pound. He pursed his lips, then produced *a shilling* and laid it beside the clothes. I did not argue – I was going to argue, but as I opened my mouth he reached out as though to take up the shilling again; I saw that I was helpless. He let me change in a small room behind the shop.[11]

Again there is the sense of an individual inhabiting a world where he is permanently at a discount – and has to apologise for it: 'I was going to argue, but . . .', 'I saw that I was helpless'. He is dramatising a little the abuse he is suffering, so that when he describes in the following sentence his being allowed to use the back-room, he abases himself further and sounds humbly grateful. The passage portrays a reduction in personality which this character anticipates and participates in. He dresses himself in the clothes, mulling over the sensation at some length:

> It gives one a very strange feeling to be wearing such clothes . . . they were not merely dirty and shapeless, they had – how is one to express it? – a gracelessness, a patina of antique filth, quite different from mere shabbiness. They were the sort of clothes you see on a bootlace-seller, or a tramp.

The process of reduction is complete when he appears completely déclassé in his new and debased state:

> An hour later, in Lambeth, I saw a hang-dog man, obviously a tramp, coming towards me, and when I looked again it was myself, reflected in a shop window. The dirt was plastering my face already . . .[12]

The physical disentanglement of the two Orwells here is matched by a possible moral detachment; or, better, perhaps, by the growth of a distinct and separate moral entity. It is a detachment which is deepened aesthetically when 'Orwell' sees – and fails to recognise himself – in the shop-window reflection. By the time we hear about the dirt plastering his face we are far less likely to be thinking of Orwell the social researcher than of Edgar in *King Lear* – similarly addicted to disguise-in-dirt – planning to grime his hair with filth and elf all his hair in knots. What is clear is that Orwell is here extending the role of the documentary well beyond its characteristic contribution while taking advantage of its natural strength.

The suspicion grows, on reading this section, that losing self-respect has a certain allure for 'Orwell' and Orwell too. We may be prompted in this direction by the speed with which Orwell appears to seek bedrock again, once he returns to London. His explanation is perfunctory and not to be excused by the fact that, in reality, the London sojourn came before that in Paris. B. tells him that the 'tame imbecile' whom he was to look after had been taken abroad and would not be back for a month, concluding with, 'I suppose you can hang on till then' – which, considering that he had had to bail him out of France, was a large assumption. No more convincing is Orwell's picture of himself stunned by the unexpected intelligence:

> I was outside in the street before it even occurred to me to borrow some more money. There was a month to wait, and I had exactly nineteen and sixpence in hand. The news had taken my breath away.[13]

The 'bridge' is a flimsy one and perhaps inevitably; for to dwell on accident – or alternatively rational curiosity – as sufficient explanation for his descent to the sub-world of the tramp would be to expose its artificiality. His journey isn't strictly necessary in any practical sense but he is fascinated by the prospect of getting out of his own society by 'going down'. He is well aware that his entry into this community cannot be a contrived one, but, and it is no exaggeration to say this, such an experience is morally essential. When we know what impels him in this direction, what he is looking for and what he finds, we will have come a long way towards penetrating Orwell's inner meaning.

Frequently Orwell talks of going 'down' to the world of the tramps, and it is remarkable how often he does so literally and how vividly his writing depicts a subterranean existence lying enticingly at the feet of the outcast. Beneath the world, public and indifferent, there lies, hopefully, another world, intimate and hospitable:

> I liked the kitchen. It was a low-ceiled cellar deep underground, very hot and drowsy with coke fumes, and lighted only by the fires, which cast black velvet shadows in the corners. Ragged washing hung on strings from the ceiling. Redlit men, stevedores mostly, moved about the fires with cooking-pots; some of them were quite naked, for they had been laundering and were waiting for their clothes to dry. At night there were games of nap and draughts, and songs – 'I'm a chap what's done wrong by my parents,' was a favourite, and so was another popular song about a shipwreck. Sometimes late at night men would come in with a pail of winkles they had bought cheap, and share them out.

> There was a general sharing of food, and it was taken for granted to feed men who were out of work.[14]

The passage is typical of a certain kind of Orwell's writing. Very obviously he liked the kitchen but exactly why is concealed by the second sentence which purports to tell us. It describes the warmth and the dark intimacy of the kitchen but his self-indulgence in the romantic clichés of low ceiled cellar and black velvet shadows blurs the nature of the feelings and their source. Out of this improbable context, with arbitrary specificity, jumps the casual but genuine description of the stevedores.

What we do learn from the passage, however, is that Orwell is attracted to this ambience at a level much deeper than he allows or, possibly, even knows. Despite – or because – of its faults the writing succeeds in postulating a whole subterranean world full of varied, mysterious and slightly disreputable life, and of shared experience. Here is another underground kitchen:

> It was a large, crowded place, with accommodation for five hundred men, and a well-known rendezvous of tramps, beggars, and petty criminals. All races, even black and white, mixed in it on terms of equality. There were Indians there, and when I spoke to one of them in bad Urdu he addressed me as 'tum' – a thing to make one shudder, if it had been in India. We had got below the range of colour prejudice. One had glimpses of curious lives. Old 'Grandpa', a tramp of seventy who made his living, or a great part of it, by collecting cigarette ends and selling the tobacco at threepence an ounce. 'The Doctor' – he was a real doctor who had been struck off the register for some offence, and besides selling newspapers gave medical advice at a few pence a time. A little Chittagonian lascar, barefoot and starving. . . . A begging-letter writer, a friend of Bozo's, who wrote pathetic appeals for aid to pay for his wife's funeral, and, when a letter had taken effect, blew himself out with huge solitary gorges of bread and margarine . . . The lodging-house was an Alsatia for types like these.[15]

The fraternity has a natural, almost organic cohesion, and is proof against intrusion from the world outside – which clearly appeals to the writer. When the party of slummers pays them a visit they are simply ignored:

> By common consent everyone in the kitchen – a hundred men, perhaps – behaved as though the slummers had not existed. There they stood patiently singing and exhorting, and no more notice was taken of them than if they had been earwigs. The gentleman in the frock coat preached a sermon, but not a word of it was audible; it was drowned in the usual din of songs, oaths, and the clattering of pans. Men sat at their meals and card games three feet away from the harmonium, peaceably ignoring it. Presently the slummers gave it up and cleared out, not insulted in any way, but merely disregarded . . .[16]

In *The Road to Wigan Pier* there occurs yet another version which enlarges the significance of these retreats and the nature of Orwell's search:

> My accent did not make him stare, I noticed; he merely demanded ninepence and then showed me the way to a frowsy firelit kitchen underground. There were stevedores and navvies and a few sailors sitting about and playing draughts and drinking tea. They barely glanced at me as I entered. But this was Saturday night and a hefty young stevedore was drunk and was reeling about the room. He turned, saw me, and lurched towards me with broad red face thrust out and a dangerous-looking fishy gleam in his eyes. I stiffened myself. So the fight was coming already! The next moment the stevedore collapsed on my chest and flung his arms round my neck. ' 'ave a cup of tea, chum!' he cried tearfully; ' 'ave a cup of tea!'
>
> I had a cup of tea. It was a kind of baptism. After that my fears vanished.[17]

There is some sort of courageous self-surrender here and also fear, both suggesting the coherent moral drive of which they are cardinal aspects. The fear is very real though it is scarcely of physical violence (which accounts, perhaps, for the comic-cut sequence of the sailor's approach 'with broad red face thrust out and a dangerous-looking fishy gleam in his eyes'). A few lines earlier he tells us that he was 'still half-afraid of the working class':

> I wanted to get in touch with them, I even wanted to become one of them, but I still thought of them as alien and dangerous; going into the dark doorway of that common lodging-house seemed to me like going down into some dreadful subterranean place – a sewer full of rats, for instance. I went in fully expecting a fight. The people would spot that I was not one of themselves and immediately infer that I had come to spy on them; and they would set upon me and throw me out – that was what I expected. I felt that I had got to do it, but I did not enjoy the prospect.[18]

To compare his descent to 'going down into some dreadful subterranean place – a sewer full of rats for instance' is grossly to over-do things if the fear is simply physical. Anyone might think that he was on his way down from the Judgement Seat instead of entering a common lodging-house in Limehouse Causeway. Clearly he is drawn to this place partly *because* of the wrath that might be visited upon him. The prospect of submitting himself to such a mortification may be painful but, as the curiously extravagant and arbitrary image he chooses to epitomise it by would suggest, there is also something titillating about it. Naturally he was impelled by Duty. ('I felt that I had got to do it.')

In fact, his fear is a particularly interesting compound. He is afraid to surrender himself to these unknown forces but also afraid that he might not be admitted even to be mauled: that the inmates of this world would see at once that he was not 'one of them' and cast him out. Grateful that his accent – his guilty past – did not automatically exclude him, he is then confronted by the apparently hostile stevedore. At the right moment the tension surrounding his entry suddenly collapses when the latter flings his arms round his neck and cries ' 'Ave a cup of tea, chum'. He drinks and his fears vanish: we need hardly be told that 'it was a kind of baptism'. Baptism is what he is looking for, and not in the sense of initiation, for the larger significance of the rite – absolution from sin – is very much to the fore. The picture is a remarkably complete one: the outcast, the penitent, is driven to seek out a community, a church which, if he is admitted to it, will ease the burden of his lonely individualism, his sin, and allocate him his place in the ranks. It is a pilgrimage made more daunting by the fearsome images which his conscience raises up but he persists and wins through to his prodigal's embrace and reward:

> After that my fears vanished. Nobody questioned me, nobody showed offensive curiosity; everybody was polite and gentle and took me utterly for granted.[19]

Orwell and 'Orwell' are continually changing places throughout the book and one can only conclude that both are in search of absolution and that Orwell is not the first *homo religiosus* to look for and find it amongst the despised and destitute. His role is of course entirely passive, his presence a surrender and his objective to become identified wholly with the mass of untouchables. Writing of Tolstoy's Father Sergius who, having discovered that his asceticism is simply a form of pride, abandons his anchorite's existence to submerge himself in the mass of the people, Nicola Chiaromonte, in *The Paradox of History*, adds '. . . one might remark that disappearing into the multitude is not only a renunciation of sanctity, but of truth as well; it is an act of pure despair'.[20] To Orwell it was certainly a renunciation of one sort of truth and to that extent it is also an act of despair: but it is also a positive alternative to going it alone.

He is in search of absolution, and he achieves it by abandoning *himself*, since it is from self that he really seeks to be absolved. So deeply ingrained in him is the negative conscience that the sense of sin is altogether bound up with the sense of himself.

In this respect, one of the most informative exposures is the celebrated 'confession' in *The Road to Wigan Pier* where he is ostensibly giving an account of his reasons for leaving the Indian Police, and going 'down and out'. It is an account which cannot but leave one with a sense of dissatisfaction: everything is so pat and so glib that it leaves us convinced that we have been listening to a rationalisation, and a confused one at that:

> When I came home on leave in 1927 I was already half

determined to throw up my job, and one sniff of English air decided me. I was not going back to be a part of that evil despotism. But I wanted much more than merely to escape from my job. For five years I had been part of an oppressive system, and it had left me with a bad conscience. Innumerable remembered faces – faces of prisoner's in the dock, of men waiting in the condemned cells, of subordinates I had bullied and aged peasants I had snubbed, of servants and coolies I had hit with my fist in moments of rage (nearly everyone does these things in the East, at any rate occasionally: Orientals can be very provoking) – haunted me intolerably. I was conscious of an immense weight of guilt that I had got to expiate.

And he adds a sentence that might be meant to allay his own uneasiness as well as ours:

I suppose that sounds exaggerated; but if you do for five years a job that you thoroughly disapprove of you will probably feel the same.

It certainly sounds lame. The method of expiation also fails to ring true:

I felt that I had got to escape not merely from imperialism but from every form of man's dominion over man. I wanted to submerge myself, to get right down among the oppressed, to be one of them and on their side against their tyrants.

If Orwell had left off after 'one of them' his account might have carried more conviction for it would have allowed the essential passivity of his actual drop-out. To finish as he does makes the excercise sound like a preliminary for guerrilla warfare. In actual fact as he prolongs his self-justification, striking an even more defensive note, it turns out to mean no more than just that – to be 'one of them':

And, chiefly because I had had to think everything out in solitude, I had carried my hatred of oppression to extraordinary lengths. At that time failure seemed to me to be the only virtue. Every suspicion of self-advancement, even to 'succeed' in life to the extent of making a few hundreds a year, seemed to me spiritually ugly, a species of bullying.

So, 'in this way', (what way, we may ask), his thoughts 'turned towards the English working class': which was really a rather peculiar thing for them to do. Old Etonian though Orwell was it is difficult to believe that he could have happily equated the working class with failure, 'the only virtue'. The rest of this extraordinary paragraph needs to be quoted to show its muddle and prevarication:

> It was the first time that I had ever been really aware of the working class, and to begin with it was only because they supplied an analogy. They were the symbolic victims of injustice, playing the same part in England as the Burmese played in Burma. In Burma the issue had been quite simple. The whites were up and the blacks were down, and therefore as a matter of course one's sympathy was with the blacks. I now realized that there was no need to go as far as Burma to find tyranny and exploitation. Here in England, down under one's feet, were the submerged working class, suffering miseries which in their different way were as bad as any an Oriental ever knows. The word 'unemployment' was on everyone's lips. That was more or less new to me, after Burma, but the drivel which the middle classes were still talking ('These unemployed are all unemployables', etc., etc.) failed to deceive me. I often wonder whether that kind of stuff deceives even the fools who utter it. On the other hand I had at that time no interest in Socialism or any other economic theory. It seemed to me then – it sometimes seems to me now, for that matter – that economic injustice will stop the moment we want it to stop, and no sooner, and if we genuinely want it to stop the method adopted hardly matters.

There is, incidentally, no evidence at all here or elsewhere that in Burma Orwell's sympathy was with the blacks in any positive sense: such information as we have hardly supports such a claim. From this point, rather indistinctly, via an excuse that his knowledge of working-class conditions was so limited that when he thought of poverty he immediately thought of brute starvation and tramps, he goes on to talk of tramps:

> Therefore my mind turned immediately towards the
> extreme cases, the social outcasts: tramps, beggars, crimi-
> nals, prostitutes. These were 'the lowest of the low', and
> these were the people with whom I wanted to get in contact.

The switches in focus are exasperating: first it is failure *tout
court*, next it is failure-as-the-working-class, then poverty, then
a whole *Beggar's Opera* underworld. But the very next sentence,
curiously intense and self-sufficient, carries real conviction at
the same time as it suggests a much less political and reasoned
objective:

> What I profoundly wanted, at that time, was to find some
> way of getting out of the respectable world altogether.

This sounds as though it could have been an end in itself, and
the account which follows shows how deeply rooted in his imagination was the notion of escape, and how well nurtured:

> I meditated upon it a great deal, I even planned parts of it
> in detail; how one could sell everything, give everything
> away, change one's name and start out with no money and
> nothing but the clothes one stood up in. But in real life
> nobody ever does that kind of thing . . .

It prepares us in some measure for the last sentence of the
paragraph which makes it quite clear that the primary
impulse is not simply to atone for past political offences but,
more generally, to escape from a much more generalised
burden of sin:

> Once I had been among them and accepted by them, I
> should have touched bottom, and – this is what I felt: I was
> aware even then that it was irrational – part of my guilt
> would drop from me.[21]

The apology in parenthesis is significant. The dramatic
change of course which the earlier paragraphs purport to
explain has been anything but rationally conceived, and the
elaborate and clumsy attempt to trace it back to guilt at his

imperial past is unlikely to convince us to the contrary.* There is no reason to disbelieve him when he confesses to feeling guilty about his work with the Indian Police but his guilt is much deeper than that of an imperialist who has seen the error of his ways. That would never have provided the source for the particular quality of his response to submersion in the tramps' world:

> I was very happy. Here I was, among 'the lowest of the low', at the bedrock of the Western world! The class-bar was down, or seemed to be down. And down there in the squalid and, as a matter of fact, horribly boring subworld of the tramp I had a feeling of release, of adventure, which seems absurd when I look back, but which was sufficiently vivid at the time.[22]

Division has disappeared from the world; justice and charity reign. In fact, his whole account of his descent into the underworld as it is described in *Down and Out in Paris and London* and *The Road to Wigan Pier* is a remarkable confession. It is a large instalment in the story of a pilgrimage; of the persistent search of the soul in a soulless world. He may cerebrally disbelieve in soul but, if so, he is more than ever like the wasp he once cut in half, for he goes on hungrily seeking to fulfil the soul's needs, without, of course, ever being able fully to admit what it is he is about or postulate any hope of fulfilment†. Barbara Everett in her book on W. H. Auden already mentioned notes that when Auden became a professing Christian, he stressed in his work two elements in Christianity that most answered his needs: these were

the two polar concepts of the isolated man, seeking a

---

* Our doubts about the objectivity of his decision to go down and out are strengthened if we look at *Keep the Aspidistra Flying* published one year before *The Road to Wigan Pier*. There Orwell offers no such rationale for the moral fascination the subworld of 'tramps, beggars, criminals, prostitutes', exerts upon Gordon Comstock whose proclivities so obviously suggest Orwell's own. (See in particular pp.118–19.)

† 'Reading Mr. Malcolm Muggeridge's brilliant and depressing book, *The Thirties*, I though of a rather cruel trick I once played on a wasp. He was sucking jam on my plate and I cut him in half. He paid no attention, merely went on with his meal, while a tiny stream of jam trickled out of his severed oesophagus. Only when he tried to fly away did he grasp the dreadful thing that had happened to him. It is the same with morden man. The thing that has been cut away is his soul, and there was a period – twenty years, perhaps – during which he did not notice it. '[23]

hidden God in a world of dread that gives no evidence of
God's existence except by the *need* man feels; and of the City
of God, the immanent and inviolable community of perfect
justice and perfect charity in which all believers are
united.[24]

The comparison helps further to articulate the nature of
Orwell's moral dilemma. He is just such an isolated man on
just such a quest and for him too there is a City of God, an
inviolable community of perfect justice and charity. (Auden
sometimes calls it 'the fabulous country', Orwell 'the Golden
Country.') But for Orwell they are conditions of two different
moral orders. To be at one with this community meant the
completest abnegation of the individual self and soul – the preservation and succour of which had seemed to him literally to
provide the basis of moral life and spiritual salvation. To seek
such communion was to him an act of self-betrayal, and it will
be interesting to see how fully the later fiction accepts this
extrapolation. From the first, of course, the attraction of this
alternative order had been apparent.

From the evidence of the two books referred to in this chapter it is clear that relationship of some sort is the objective of
his search. This is explicit in the recurrent image of the figure
hovering just outside the circle of light and warmth, grateful to
be admitted yet never fully assimilated; the figure not blessed
but cursed by the observing eye which can reveal things to him
only in their objectivity – a method of knowledge not of feeling, of alienation (by its necessary definition of his individuality) not of sympathy. And there is, of course, no chance of
Orwell settling for the Kiplingesque solution of relationship
between autonomous groups. To him relationship means ega-
litarian fusion, for in no other way can that fluid intimacy he
so desired be reached. In this connection, his experience in the
East had impressed him, with its conspicuous absence of
class-consciousness. A high native official in order to make his
presence felt at a wayside inn might bluster and call everybody names, but, his dignity asserted, he will sit down 'in perfect amity with the baggage coolies' without any feeling that
they are 'of different clay from himself'. Orwell concludes
rather enviously:

I have observed countless similar scenes in Burma. Among Mongolians – among all Asiatics, for all I know – there is a sort of natural equality, an easy intimacy between man and man, which is simply unthinkable in the West.[25]

Unthinkable or not it is just such an intimacy that he is seeking. The major barrier in England is the class-system which becomes for Orwell intensely personal, reflecting something more than the class-division which offends his social conscience. He is deeply conscious of being on the other side of the barrier and, by his very existence, perpetuating it. When he seeks entry to the tramps' world he is certain that his accent will give him away:

> I cannot, for instance, disguise my accent, at any rate not for more than a very few minutes. I imagined – notice the frightful class-consciousness of the Englishman – that I should be spotted as a 'gentleman' the moment I opened my mouth; . . .[26]

He tells us the same story in *Down and Out in Paris and London*:

> Dressed as I was, I was half afraid that the police might arrest me as a vagabond, and I dared not speak to anyone, imagining that they must notice a disparity between my accent and my clothes.[27]

He need not have worried, of course. When he sought a bed from the 'deputy' of the cheap lodging-house, we might recall, no questions had been asked: 'My accent did not make him stare, I noticed; he merely demanded ninepence.'

The denial of his expectations leaves an impression almost of disappointment. Certainly he is immensely conscious of accent as a barrier, and here it proves not to be one. For all that there are a number of instances when his 'difference' is satisfactorily betrayed. In another cheap lodging-house a drunken fellow-resident assumes from his accent that he is, like himself, an ex-public schoolboy and obligingly sings him the Eton boating-song; while a gentleman-picnicker, surprising him in conversation into forgetting his assumed cockney, presses a shilling upon him in embarrassed recognition of his fallen state.

Given his sensitivity on this subject, Orwell is at times a little careless. In an exchange in a 'spike', for instance, his gentleman's expostulation hardly chimes with his surroundings:

> I looked round the cell with a vague feeling that there was something missing. Then, with a shock of surprise, I realized what it was, and exclaimed:
>
> 'But I say, damn it, where are the beds?'
>
> '*Beds?*' said the other man, surprised. 'There aren't no beds! What yer expect? This is one of them spikes where you sleeps on the floor . . .'[28]

When he is speaking to us, his readers, his vocabulary and tone are defiantly and incongruously class-conscious: as if the accusatory voice might come from us when it didn't come from any other quarter.

> Other tramps were arriving by ones and twos. It was jolly autumn weather . . .
>
> Once again it was jolly autumn weather, and the road was quiet, with few cars passing . . .
>
> '. . . The stars are a free show; it don't cost anything to use your eyes.'
>
> 'What a good idea! I should never have thought of it.'
>
> I gave my trade as 'painter'; I had painted watercolours – who has not?[29]

At times his class-difference is rumbled without, apparently, his saying a word. There is an interesting discrepancy between his description of such an exposure in *Down and Out in Paris and London* and his earlier description of the incident in an article for 'The Adelphi'. In the former Orwell tells us that on entering the 'spike' he had given his trade as journalist. The Tramp Major supervising the 'spike' calls his name:

> 'So you are a journalist?' 'Yes, sir,' I said, quaking. A few questions would betray the fact that I had been lying,

which might mean prison. But the Tramp Major only looked me up and down and said: 'Then you are a gentleman?' 'I suppose so.' He gave me another long look. 'Well that's bloody bad luck, guv'nor,' he said: 'bloody bad luck that is'. And thereafter he treated me with unfair favouritism, and even with a kind of deference.[30]

(It is interesting that it should be this more elaborated version which has any reference to his 'quaking' and his fear of prosecution.)

The other account makes his disguise seem even more easily penetrated:

[The Tramp Major] was a gruff, soldierly man of forty, who gave the tramps no more ceremony than sheep at the dipping-pond, shoving them this way and that and shouting oaths in their faces. But when he came to myself, he looked hard at me, and said:

'You are a gentleman?'

'I suppose so,' I said.

He gave me another long look, "Well that's bloody bad luck guv'nor,' he said, 'that's bloody bad luck, that is.' And thereafter he took it into his head to treat me with compassion, even with a kind of respect.[31]

Class, it seems, will out: like guilt.

The class-system is, to Orwell, a barrier, designed to keep people apart; as such it is in his work less a socio-political phenomenon than the reflection of his own moral self-division. That the crisis is deep within himself we might suspect from his preoccupation with his own status but it is confirmed strongly in his almost hysterical revulsion *towards* those on the other side of the divide. He recognises that he is cut off from the working-class and appreciates that his education and his parents' snobbery had a good deal to do with this. But what he then goes on to exhibit is an emotional revulsion so intense that it certainly could never have been taught:

. . . it was not long before I was forbidden to play with the plumber's children; they were 'common' and I was told to keep away from them. This was snobbish, if you like, but it was also necessary, for middle-class people cannot afford to let their children grow up with vulgar accents. So, very early, the working class ceased to be a race of friendly and wonderful beings and became a race of enemies.[32]

This is ambiguous enough but then there comes a further explanation:

> But there was another and more serious difficulty. Here you come to the real secret of class distinctions in the West – the real reason why a European of bourgeois upbringing, even when he calls himself a Communist, cannot without a hard effort think of a working man as his equal. It is summed up in four frightful words which people nowadays are chary of uttering, but which were bandied about quite freely in my childhood. The words were: *the lower classes smell.*

And, of course, this is something gratifyingly beyond one's ability to exorcise:

> . . . here, obviously, you are at an impassable barrier. For no feeling of like or dislike is quite so fundamental as a *physical* feeling. Race-hatred, religious hatred, differences of education, of temperament, of intellect, even differences of moral code, can be got over; but physical repulsion cannot. You can have an affection for a murderer or a sodomite, but you cannot have an affection for a man whose breath stinks – habitually stinks, I mean. However well you may wish him, however much you may admire his mind and character, if his breath stinks he is horrible and in your heart of hearts you will hate him.

The vigour of his attack again recalls Swift: but it also recalls something else. From the twelfth to the sixteenth centuries the analogy by which the coherence of society had been described was that of the human body, only discarded, as Tawney has indicated, with the rise of theoretical individualism in the seventeenth century. There is therefore an apt, if involuted, irony in this latter-day Puritan projecting his own self-division and self-repugnance in terms of class-division –

and then discovering that this last is rooted in a physical aversion.

His claim at the end of that passage of universality for his phobia is hardly strengthened by what follows:

> Very early in life you acquired the idea that there was something subtly repulsive about a working-class body; you would not get nearer to it than you could help. You watched a great sweaty navvy walking down the road with his pick over his shoulder; you looked at his discoloured shirt and his corduroy trousers stiff with the dirt of a decade; you thought of those nests and layers of greasy rags below, and, under all, the unwashed body, brown all over (that was how I used to imagine it), with its strong, bacon-like reek.[33]

Clearly his imagination was intensely active. There is either disingenuousness or a remarkable lack of self-awareness in the rationale that follows:

> Everyone who has grown up pronouncing his aitches and in a house with a bathroom and one servant is likely to have grown up with these feelings; hence the chasmic, impassable quality of class-distinctions in the West.

He goes on to quote Somerset Maugham as the one just man who has testified to the truth he has proposed. But one only needs to juxtapose Maugham's comment with Orwell's description of the navvy to perceive the immense difference between them:

> In the West we are divided from our fellows by our sense of smell. The working man is our master, inclined to rule us with an iron hand, but it cannot be denied that he stinks: none can wonder at it, for a bath in the dawn when you have to hurry to your work before the factory bell rings is no pleasant thing, nor does heavy labour tend to sweetness; and you do not change your linen more than you can help when the week's washing must be done by a sharp-tongued wife. I do not blame the working man because he stinks, but stink he does. It makes social intercourse difficult to persons of sensitive nostril. The matutinal tub divides the classes

more effectively than birth, wealth or education.[34]

The irony is considerable; the condescending Maugham's cool detachment shows up so fully Orwell's obsessive preoccupation.

For Orwell to expound class-distinction not in terms of economics nor of the accident of birth, but of an obsessive aversion, an irrational phobia, suggests just how far this issue might have been taken over and directed by his own moral self-division. To ascribe the source of class distinction as he does is of course to make it part of one's nature and all the more ineradicable; it is indeed to make it 'an impassable barrier'. There is another implication: while placing the source of class-consciousness beyond the range of rational challenge, his identification of it as a defect of nature gives it something of the status of original sin – at any rate it is an involuntary, received condition for which, nevertheless, one cannot disown responsibility.

But the feeling is not just 'a feeling': it is a nasty smell. The senses are of the first importance to Orwell but it is the olfactory sense which brings to him the stink of corruption – and a sense-impression is not the same as revelation: it is not disembodied for it belongs uncompromisingly to the individual and it cannot be disowned. Is it unfair to assume from this that it is part of his humanity, the corrupt and corruptible part, spiritual and physical, that Orwell is revolted by? It seems to me that this is implicit, for example, in the description of his attitude to his Burmese servant:

> When you have a lot of servants you soon get into lazy habits, and I habitually allowed myself, for instance, to be dressed and undressed by my Burmese boy. This was because he was a Burman and undisgusting; I could not have endured to let an English manservant handle me in that intimate manner. I felt towards a Burman almost as I felt towards a woman. Like most other races, the Burmese have a distinctive smell – I cannot describe it; it is a smell that makes one's teeth tingle – but this smell never disgusted me. (Incidentally, Orientals say that *we* smell. The Chinese, I believe, say that a white man smells like a corpse. The Burmese say the same – though no Burman

was ever rude enough to say so to me.)[35]

It is clear here, not because the self-exposure is unconscious but just because it is so highly *conscious*. What else can the mannered Swiftian sentence signify ('I could not have endured to let an English manservant handle me in that intimate manner'). Orwell is playing Gulliver to their deodorised Houyhnhnms, even to the extent of apologetically reflecting on the offence he must be giving them. And he is playing to the gallery; challenging us a little dramatically, and with some of that emotional extravagance so often lying just beneath his verbal restraint, to note the extremity of his disgust.

In one respect he is too successful in evoking Swift. When a little later he attempts to write it all down to pure, doctrinal class-prejudice, what sticks with us is the intimately subjective nature of his response and not the attempt to explain it away:

> Of course I admired and liked the private soldiers as any youth of twenty would admire and like hefty, cheery youths five years older than himself with the medals of the Great War on their chests. And yet, after all, they faintly repelled me; they were 'common people' and I did not care to be too close to them. In the hot mornings when the company marched down the road, myself in the rear with one of the junior subalterns, the steam of those hundred sweating bodies in front made my stomach turn. And this, you observe, was pure prejudice. For a soldier is probably as inoffensive, physically, as it is possible for a male white person to be. He is generally young, he is nearly always healthy from fresh air and exercise, and a rigorous discipline compels him to be clean. But I could not see it like that. All I knew was that it was *lower-class* sweat that I was smelling, and the thought of it made me sick.[36]

The attitude in these passages is surely very nearly that of Swift towards the Yahoos whom he saw as images of the fallen state of man, corrupt, foul and stinking.

Orwell altogether imbues the form of class-distinction with his own spiritual and moral crisis. It becomes a barrier which he himself has created out of his own basic self-division to epitomise that self-division. It dramatises a world, loathsome and repellent, distinct from his other world and separated from it by a wall. But it is a glass wall which allows – even encourages – a full view while at the same time cutting him off:

> Whichever way you turn this curse of class-difference confronts you like a wall of stone. Or rather it is not so much like a stone wall as the plate-glass pane of an aquarium; it is so easy to pretend that it isn't there, and so impossible to get through it.[37]

We are reminded again of his earlier description of the woman clearing the blocked pipe – viewed through the window of the train.

What might be described as a species of spiritual voyeurism pervades Orwell's writing and is, of course, a significant part of the moral pattern. He cannot take his eyes off the glass wall and what he sees on the other side, but greater familiarity with what is beyond can be achieved only in over-excited, not to say lurid, projections. This, however, is precisely the reality those repellent figures have, for they, too, are the external projection of his self-division.

Epitomised in class-distinction, then, this self-division appears as an inseparable part of human nature and as such is closely analogous, to put it no stronger, with the concept of original sin. Moreover it is an analogue strengthened by the realisation that class-distinction symptomises not just the inherent sin but also the guilt. In his inmost self Orwell accepts responsibility both for the division and for what, offensive as it is, lies on the other side as its product; all that is loathly and corrupt in the physically human. Further, he also sees it as his responsibility to redeem his guilt.

So we get *The Road to Wigan Pier*: a pilgrim's road, as the all-important second half makes clear. The first section conveys the initial impression of a documentary, if one with some peculiarly resonant vignettes, but the second half with its emphasis on guilt and expiation and its laboured account of how the latter came to be concerned with the working-class, offers a quite different perspective on the whole book. We become aware of Orwell himself as prismatic 'Orwell' through whose particular moral consciousness – exposed for us in the Mandalay section – the Wigan experience is refracted. As the book progresses the realisation grows in us that it is primarily to be seen neither as a blue-book on working class conditions in the north of England nor as a social historian's travelogue but, in its own minor way, as a Baedeker of the soul.

Every one of George Orwell's books is centrally concerned with crossing a barrier, a barrier which, in the end, divides man from himself. And in every case but one the protagonist retreats behind it, unfulfilled. It is so much easier simply to accept the division, and the guilt, and the torture of the negative conscience, than to risk the dangers inherent in abolishing the barrier which would entail full acceptance of responsibility for the original sin, *and for re-integration.*

To the Puritan conscience in particular such development presents an acute if not, indeed, an insuperable problem. The identity the Puritan achieves is nothing if not individual and it is gained ultimately in isolation from his fellowmen. It is an identity which thrives on exclusiveness and indeed sustains its brittle integrity by means of distinctions and barriers. For Orwell to erase the barrier is to lose that identity and to leave himself with only one alternative – the identity of sinner who can only passively wait in the hope of absolution.

In all his accounts of his association with the outcast and the working-class, he shows a sharp awareness of his own middle-class 'difference'. So that in his many attempts to make friends with 'the lowest of the low' there is a reservation, an area which is uncommitted, a consciousness of his being apart from the people he is among. This gives him an identity which the abolition of the barrier would destroy:

> The fact that has got to be faced is that to abolish class-distinction means abolishing a part of yourself. Here am I, a typical member of the middle class. It is easy for me to say that I want to get rid of class-distinctions, but nearly everything I think and do is a result of class-distinctions. All my notions – notions of good and evil, of pleasant and unpleasant, of funny and serious, of ugly and beautiful – are essentially *middle-class* notions; my taste in books and food and clothes, my sense of honour, my table manners, my turns of speech, my accent, even the characteristic movements of my body, are the product of a special kind of

> upbringing and a special niche about half-way up the social
> hierarchy . . . to get outside the class-racket I have got to
> suppress not merely my private snobbishness, but most of
> my other tastes and prejudices as well. I have got to alter
> myself so completely that at the end I should hardly be
> recognizable as the same person.[38]

Abolishing the division means giving up a *moral* position and if
one's whole integrity has been built round the principle such a
position embodies, to relinquish it is to relinquish the achieved
identity: one will no longer 'be recognizable as the same
person'. And Orwell is caught in the dilemma. He reveals the
division as self-created and his consciousness of the resultant
alienation. He also reveals his longing for re-integration and
his guilt in not achieving it. From this follows all his sad pere-
grinations, seeking incorporation with what lies beyond the
division: his conscientious attempts to render himself unrecog-
nisable as the same person by his self-conscious adoption of
disguise; his characteristically over-ready identification:

> She talked upon religious subjects – about Jesus Christ
> always having a soft spot for poor rough men like us, and
> about how quickly the time passed when you were in
> church, and what a difference it made to a man on the road
> if he said his prayers regularly. We hated it. We sat against
> the wall fingering our caps (a tramp feels indecently
> exposed with his cap off), and turning pink and trying to
> mumble something when the lady addressed us.[39]

There are brief moments when he comes near to acquiring
the alternative identity but he is in the position of him who to
gain his life must lose it, and up to the last book there is an
ultimate reluctance to go all the way. Nor is this surprising for
to cross the barrier is to submerge that hard-won, combative
individualism in the quietist identity of the sinner who has
accepted the fact that reliance on his own efforts to earn or justify absolution is useless. It is to submit to something which
will destroy him; to submit himself to those horrors of the imagination he himself has created as a substitute for a full confrontation of his guilt and sin. (The rats, for example, in *The
Road to Wigan Pier* and *Nineteen Eighty-Four*.) It is to submit

himself to punishment, and, worse still, to the possibility of
repudiation:

> . . . you see I was still half afraid of the working class. I
> wanted to get in touch with them, I even wanted to become
> one of them, but I still thought of them as alien and dan-
> gerous . . .
> They would spot that I was not one of themselves and
> immediately infer that I had come to spy on them; and they
> would set upon me and throw me out – that was what I
> expected.

Once over the threshold, however, and compassed in the
larger integrity he will achieve a place, fulfilled in the 'utter
equality' (so heavily stressed) of his new relationship; but it
will, of course, be a squalid egalitarianism compared with his
former heroic individualism:

> Once you are in that world and seemingly *of* it, it hardly
> matters what you have been in the past. It is a sort of world-
> within-a-world where everyone is equal, a small squalid
> democracy – perhaps the nearest thing to a democracy that
> exists in England.[40]

Undoubtedly his going down to 'the bedrock of the Western
world' was an attempt at exorcism but in *The Road to Wigan
Pier*, Orwell is still stopping short of complete admission as to
the true, highly personal, nature of his purpose – or of his
crisis. The result is an almost bland espousal of 'objectivity'
and the empirical stance, while the language simultaneously
(and often incongruously) betrays the powerful and highly
subjective vested interest. It is rather like one ascetic dis-
interestedly, recommending to another the homeopathic
benefits of a good scourging:

> A working man's body, as such, is no more repulsive to me
> than a millionaire's. I still don't like drinking out of a cup or
> bottle after another person – another man, I mean; with
> women I don't mind – but at least the question of class does
> not enter. It was rubbing shoulders with the tramps that
> cured me of it. Tramps are not really very dirty as English
> people go, but they have the name for being dirty, and
> when you have shared a bed with a tramp and drunk tea

> out of the same snuff-tin, you feel that you have seen the
> worst and the worst has no terrors for you.[41]

At this point he is still talking about immunisation rather than
conversion.

*　　*　　*

Guilt and expiation form a dominant theme in *The Road to
Wigan Pier*, but to appreciate just how deep-rooted in Orwell
was the sense of irredeemable sin one must turn to his long
essay on his childhood, 'Such, Such Were the Joys', written
many years after the event in the early part of 1947. The date
is important: whether or not things were as they are described, Orwell, in his early forties, saw them in this light.

It is a remarkable account and the degree to which it makes
explicit so much that has been said here about Orwell's preoccupation with guilt and sin is astonishing. After reading it,
it is impossible to think of the guilt described in *The Road to
Wigan Pier* as emanating from his consciousness of an imperialist past:

> From the age of eight, or even earlier, the consciousness of
> sin was never far away from me. If I contrived to seem cal-
> lous and defiant, it was only a thin cover over a mass of
> shame and dismay.[42]

The essay is, of course, concerned with life at his odious prep-
school, 'St. Cyprian's', where the brutality of the treatment
meted out – in particular to cure him of bed-wetting – undoubtedly exaggerated his sense of guilt and self-disgust:

> I knew that the bed-wetting was (a) wicked and (b) outside
> my control. The second fact I was personally aware of, and
> the first I did not question. It was possible, therefore, to
> commit a sin without knowing that you committed it,
> without wanting to commit it, and without being able to
> avoid it. Sin was not necessarily something that you did: it
> might be something that happened to you. I do not want to
> claim that this idea flashed into my mind as a complete
> novelty at this very moment, under the blows of Sambo's
> cane: I must have had glimpses of it even before I left home,
> for my early childhood had not been altogether happy. But

at any rate this was the great, abiding lesson of my boyhood: that I was in a world where it was *not possible* for me to
be good. And the double beating was a turning-point, for it
brought home to me for the first time the harshness of the
environment into which I had been flung. Life was more
terrible, and I was more wicked, than I had imagined. At
any rate, as I sat snivelling on the edge of a chair in
Sambo's study, with not even the self-possession to stand
up while he stormed at me, I had a conviction of sin and
folly and weakness, such as I do not remember to have felt
before.[43]

Orwell knows of course, that such a discriminating and articulate critique can't be passed off as the reflections of a ten-year
old; but he will not have it that this diminishes its auth-
enticity:

In general, one's memories of any period must necessarily
weaken as one moves away from it . . . But it can also
happen that one's memories grow sharper after a long lapse
of time, because one is looking at the past with fresh eyes
and can isolate and, as it were, notice facts which previous-
ly existed undifferentiated amongst a mass of others.[44]

The manner in which the older Orwell now structures these
earlier experiences is of great importance to us: and always it
comes back to self-disgust and sin:

. . . the WC and dirty handkerchief side of life is necessarily
more obtrusive when great numbers of human beings are
crushed together in a small space . . . Besides, boyhood is
the age of disgust. After one has learned to differentiate,
and before one has become hardened – between seven and
eighteen, say – one seems always to be walking the tight-
rope over a cesspool.[45]

The equation of physical filth and moral delinquency is, as
we readily recognise by this time, entirely characteristic of the
mature Orwell, but again in this extraordinary generalisation
(and its imagery) one can see how deeply ingrained was the
notion and how organic in its development.

But it is the sense of moral delinquency, of sin, which

dominates. At one point it is given clear shape when St. Cyprian's launches a massive pogrom against masturbators. Then 'Guilt seemed to hang in the air like a cloud of smoke'. Orwell, totally unaware of the cause of the fuss and totally innocent of the charge, is nevertheless included in the circle of the sinners by the master who, *ex post facto*, is delivering a talk on the Temple of the Body:

> He turned his cavernous black eyes on me and added sadly: 'And you, whom I'd always believed to be quite a decent person after your fashion – you, I hear, are one of the very worst.'
> A feeling of doom descended upon me. So I was guilty too. I too had done the dreadful thing, whatever it was, that wrecked you for life, body and soul, and ended in suicide or the lunatic asylum. Till then I had hoped that I was innocent, and the conviction of sin which now took possession of me was perhaps all the stronger because I did not know what I had done.[46]

The last part of the last sentence might suggest an adult rationale but in any event it underlines Orwell's preocuppation with a sense of *inherent* sin. In this childhood world it was not possible to be good since pervasive sinfulness was liable to break out in you at any moment whatever your intention: essentially you were corrupt:

> . . . all his folly, wickedness and ingratitude, it seemed, was inescapable, because I lived among laws which were absolute, like the law of gravity, but which it was not possible for me to keep.[47]

This clearly transcends the observation of childhood, for only an experienced and weary sensibility could so formulate a central dilemma of the *homo religiosus*. (It is a formulation which gains added significance if we consider that at the time Orwell was in the middle of *Nineteen Eighty-Four*.)

The problem is one which Luther did much to intensify with his insistence on the importance of the divine law and his equally strong insistence on its correlative of divine wrath. This new emphasis on the Pauline doctrine of 'wrath' as a reality in God meant, as J. S. Whale points out in *The Protestant*

Tradition, 'a new turn of thought, not only about God, but also about his world'. Whale goes on, giving a context that is illuminating to the general argument of this study, to make clear the outcome of this emphasis in a pessimistic near-defeatism:

> The thought of the Christian centuries had constantly been influenced, and sometimes menaced, by the Platonist mysticism which would see the world and its history as no more than a copy or shadow of the Real – time itself being but the moving image of the Eternal. But in saying that God is wrathful, Luther was again vindicating the reality and independence of God's creation. The world of man is real, and responsible to God its maker and judge. The moral law, which demands absolute realisation, once again becomes the only valid norm of thought about the world.
> But for Luther this thought is always twofold. It is as terrifying as it is sublime. He sees that only the perfect may stand before him 'who is of purer eyes than to behold iniquity'. He sees, too, that no one can; for 'there is none righteous, no not one'.[48]

Later Whale succinctly redefines the dilemma: 'what man, as man, must do is what man, as sinner, cannot do'.[49]

Orwell himself comes very near saying this in so many words:

> I did not question the prevailing standards, because so far as I could see there were no others . . .
> And yet from a very early age I was aware of the impossibility of any *subjective* conformity. Always at the centre of my heart the inner self seemed to be awake, pointing out the difference between the moral obligation and the psychological *fact* . . .
> It was not that one did not want to possess the right qualities or feel the correct emotions, but that one could not. The good and the possible never seemed to coincide.[50]

Here another image will intrude for those familiar with Orwell's last book: that of Winston Smith grovelling before O'Brien, assuring him that he would see five fingers if he possibly could – and meaning it.

Occasionally, we are told in the essay, there would be

moments of a sort of dumb defiance when Orwell would
accept, even relish, his sinfulness. How far this is a genuine
memory is not really of great importance: it is clear enough
from the evidence in *Down and Out in Paris and London* and *The
Road to Wigan Pier* to take only two books, that this, too, is an
integral part of his response to experience:

> Over a period of about two years, I do not think there was
> ever a day when 'the exam', as I called it, was quite out of
> my waking thoughts . . .
> And yet curiously enough I was also tormented by an
> almost irresistible impulse *not* to work . . . in term time.
> also, I would go through periods of idleness and stupidity
> when I would sink deeper into disgrace and even achieve a
> sort of feeble, snivelling defiance, fully conscious of my guilt
> and yet unable or unwilling – I could not be sure which – to
> do any better.[51]

It is a picture that has a good deal in common with that of
Gordon Comstock in *Keep the Aspidistra Flying* drawing comfort
from the apparently irredeemable position he had got himself
into.

If his familiarity with the psychology of the negative conscience dates back to his childhood, so too, it would appear,
does his instinctive understanding of the psychology of the
victim. Guilt and acceptance of righteous persecution go together in this reprise of life at St. Cyprian's:

> I have said that at St. Cyprian's we were not allowed to
> keep our own money. However, it was possible to hold back
> a shilling or two, and sometimes I used furtively to buy
> sweets which I kept hidden in the loose ivy on the playing-
> field wall. One day when I had been sent on an errand I
> went into a sweet-shop a mile or more from the school and
> bought some chocolates. As I came out of the shop I saw on
> the opposite pavement a small sharp-faced man who
> seemed to be staring very hard at my school cap. Instantly a
> horrible fear went through me. There could be no doubt as
> to who the man was. He was a spy placed there by Sambo!
> I turned away unconcernedly, and then, as though my legs
> were doing it of their own accord, broke into a clumsy run.

But when I got round the next corner I forced myself to walk again, for to run was a sign of guilt, and obviously there would be other spies posted here and there about the town. All that day and the next I waited for the summons to the study, and was surprised when it did not come. It did not seem to me strange that the headmaster of a private school should dispose of an army of informers, and I did not even imagine that he would have to pay them. I assumed that any adult, inside the school or outside, would collaborate voluntarily in preventing us from breaking the rules. Sambo was all-powerful; it was natural that his agents should be everywhere.[52]

It is extraordinary the way in which the 'young' Orwell has created a totalitarian microcosm out of the world of his school – a world where 'To survive, or at least to preserve any kind of independence, was essentially criminal, since it meant breaking rules which you yourself recognised'. The only identity left, it seems was that of the sinner. The isolation and the moral confusion which Orwell perceptively saw as the techniques of totalitarianism are central to his experiences here too:

> the sense of desolate loneliness and helplessness, of being locked up not only in a hostile world but in a world of good and evil where the rules were such that it was actually not possible for me to keep them.[53]

To accept as the only identity that of the sinner is, Erik Erikson reminds us, to make '[man's] status and inner state totally dependent on the monopolists of salvation'.[54] The best description of this is, of course, *Nineteen Eighty-four*, but it comes out well (and contemporarily) in Orwell's over.confessional description of the schoolboy victim's mixture of hatred and servility:

> The high-water mark of good favour was to be invited to serve at table on Sunday nights when Flip and Sambo had guests to dinner. In clearing away, of course, one had a chance to finish off the scraps, but one also got a servile pleasure from standing behind the seated guests and darting deferentially forward when something was wanted.

Whenever one had the chance to suck up, one did suck up, and at the first smile one's hatred turned into a sort of cringing love. I was always tremendously proud when I succeeded in making Flip laugh . . .

And yet all the while, at the middle of one's heart, there seemed to stand an incorruptible inner self who knew that whatever one did — whether one laughed or snivelled or went into frenzies of gratitude for small favours — one's only true feeling was hatred.[55]

*   *   *

When Erik Erikson asserts that Luther 'rejected all arrangements by which an assortment of saints made it unnecessary for man to embrace the maximum of his own existential suffering', and adds that Luther had made a virtue out of what his superiors had considered a vice in him 'namely, the determined search for the rock bottom of sinfulness',[56] we are again very forcibly reminded of Orwell's tormenting sense of guilt and the nature and force of his drive to reach 'the bedrock of the Western world'. The identity is obviously much more than semantic.

Orwell does indeed go down and out in order to embrace the maximum of his own existential suffering: his fear and his revulsion at going beyond the barrier are genuine but his drive to do so is insistent. There is no doubt that he finds human physicality fundamentally distressing and his observer's eye seems — inevitably — fitted with a zoom-lens to increase the intimacy and magnify the grossness:

> The old woman made off, mumbling, with malevolence in the hump of her shoulders, and joined her husband. He paused on the kerb to cough, so fruitily that you could hear him through the door. A clot of phlegm, like a little white tongue, came slowly out between his lips and was ejected into the gutter. Then the two old creatures shuffled away, beetle-like in the long greasy overcoats that hid everything except their feet.[57]

Nevertheless, he cannot deny this physicality, ultimately his own, and he returns to it obsessively time and again. The Brookers, in *The Road to Wigan Pier*, are described as living in the extreme of squalor with meticulous attention given to every disgusting detail, yet one can't simply shrug them off and forget about them: and not just because of their numbers as he suggests:

It was not only the dirt, the smells, and the vile food, but the feeling of stagnant meaningless decay, of having got down into some subterranean place where people go creeping round and round, just like black beetles, in an endless muddle of slovened jobs and mean grievances. The most dreadful thing about people like the Brookers is the way they say the same things over and over again. It gives you the feeling that they are not real people at all, but a kind of ghost for ever rehearsing the same futile rigmarole. . . . But it is no use saying that people like the Brookers are just disgusting and trying to put them out of mind. For they exist in tens and hundreds of thousands; they are one of the characteristic by-products of the modern world. You cannot disregard them if you accept the civilization that produced them. . . . It is a kind of duty to see and smell such places now and again, especially smell them, lest you should forget that they exist; though perhaps it is better not to stay there too long. [58]

It *is* a duty and one of a fundamental moral order, for it is a reminder, not just that the Brookers exist, but that there is an aspect of humanity which is beetle-like, which seems, in its stink and squalor, to have crept out of a hole in the ground — and which must for all that, indeed just because of all that since it is one's own responsibility and condition, be fully acknowledged.

To face this squarely is to accept a moral truth about human nature and the human condition that it is divided against itself and that man is both a reflection and the cause of that division. Only by facing his resultant negative conscience without evasion can his sin be expiated and an identity discovered. In practical terms this entailed Orwell crossing the self-created barrier, giving up the identity which the barrier had allowed him and finding another by incorporating himself in the larger integrity. But this means not just becoming one of the lowest of the low but, in his case, accepting the passive identity of the sinner.

Thus we have an equation of the social outcasts – cut off by the barrier of their poverty from the rest of society – with the sinner, which is what gives the peculiar moral density to Orwell's repeated efforts to get down to bed-rock and to his preoccupation with degradation and poverty. When he has Gordon Comstock quote from the Prologue to the Man of Lawe's Tale. 'If thou be poure thy brother hateth thee' (echoing, as Orwell no doubt knew from his extensive reading of the bible. Proverbs XIX:4 'All the brethren of the poore do hate him'), he is describing both the alienation of the poor and the moral obliquity involved in poverty. Elsewhere he notes that 'The English are a conscience-ridden race, with a strong sense of the sinfulness of poverty'.[59] But it is an obliquity which both Comstock and Orwell welcome. After all, if men hate you then your condition of sinfulness – or at any rate your moral and social inferiority – is being recognised. You are one of a despised and rejected sub-caste – but at least you have *that* identity. This dual moral and psychological reality is undoubtedly what Orwell discovers in the world of the poor and the down-and-out. Altogether typically he insists on an almost Platonic identity of physical and moral degradation. When Ravelston objects to Comstock's quotation because "People don't hate you, exactly', he gets this uncompromising reply:

> They do. And they're quite right to hate you. You *are* hateful. It's like those ads for Listerine. 'Why is he always alone? Halitosis is ruining his career.' Poverty is spiritual halitosis.[60]

The persecution which the degradation of poverty (and sin?) attracts is a theme which gets a lot of emphasis in the book. Comstock justifies it in the previous quotation and welcomes it in this:

> He clung with a sort of painful joy to the notion that because he was poor everyone must *want* to insult him.[61]

One must remind oneself not to confuse Comstock and Orwell but these quotations are so much in the idiom of other pieces that no violence is being done to the novel in suggesting an identity here.

Conversely there is an envious yearning after the physical grace of the privileged as though in it was represented grace of a higher order:

Though [Ravelston] was a year older than Gordon he looked much younger. He was very tall, with a lean, wide-shouldered body and the typical lounging grace of the upper-class youth.[62]

Or again:

Gordon knew his type. The moneyed 'artistic' young man. Not an artist himself, exactly, but a hanger-on of the arts; frequenter of studios, retailer of scandal. A nice-looking boy, though, for all his Nancitude. The skin at the back of his neck was as silky-smooth as the inside of a shell. You can't have a skin like that under five hundred a year. A sort of charm he had, a glamour, like all moneyed people. Money and charm; who shall separate them?[63]

The inaccessibility of this world and its capacity to attract and repel is caught for Comstock as he is walking back to his dreary lodgings:

Another shoal of cars swam past. One in particular caught his eye, a long slender thing, elegant as a swallow, all gleaming blue and silver; a thousand guineas it would have cost, he thought. A blue-clad chauffeur sat at the wheel, upright, immobile, like some scornful statue. At the back, in the pink-lit interior, four elegant young people, two youths, and two girls, were smoking cigarettes and laughing. He had a glimpse of sleek bunny-faces; faces of ravishing pinkness and smoothness, lit by that peculiar inner glow that can never be counterfeited, the soft warm radiance of money.[64]

It is an interesting paradox (though now, I think, intelligible) that the writer for whom direct contact with the 'real' world around him was a moral necessity, should, so often, see that world as something akin to a prison sub-divided and surrounded by walls of glass.

Keep the Aspidistra Flying is also a description of going down and out but affluence and materialism are being positively and explicitly repudiated here, and with doctrinal vigour. Unhappily it is a very muddled book and while poverty is equated with a purifying, anchoretic rebellion, it is also being continually equated with a state of hopeless sinfulness and a submissive renunciation of all personal responsibility and authority. Gordon Comstock decides to opt out of society where 'Money-worship [had] been elevated into a religion'. He tells himself that he needs freedom to develop his literary talent, but he is aware that this is an excuse:

> . . . it was not the desire to 'write' that was his real motive. To get out of the money-world – that was what he wanted. Vaguely he looked forward to some kind of money-less, anchorite existence.[65]

What he ultimately comes to seek is the complete abdication of responsibility and a totally passive existence:

> Under ground, under ground! Down in the safe soft womb of earth, where there is no getting of jobs or losing of jobs, no relatives or friends to plague you, no hope, fear, ambition, honour, duty – no *duns* of any kind. That was where he wished to be.
> Yet is was not death, actual physical death, that he wished for. It was a queer feeling that he had. It had been with him ever since that morning when he had woken up in the police cell. The evil, mutinous mood that comes after drunkenness seemed to have set into a habit. That drunken night had marked a period in his life. It had dragged him downward with strange suddenness. Before, he had fought against the money-code, and yet he had clung to his wretched remnant of decency. But now it was precisely from decency that he wanted to escape. He wanted to go down, deep down, into some world where decency no longer mattered; to cut the strings of his self-respect, to submerge himself – to *sink*, as Rosemary had said. It was all bound up in his mind with the thought of being *under ground*. He liked to think about the lost people, the under ground people, tramps, beggars, criminals, prostitutes. It is a good world that they inhabit, down there in their frowzy kips and spikes. He liked to think that beneath the world of money there is that great

sluttish underworld where failure and success have no meaning; a sort of kingdom of ghosts where all are equal. That was where he wished to be, down in the ghost-kingdom, *below* ambition. It comforted him somehow to think of the smoke-dim slums of South London sprawling on and on, a huge graceless wilderness where you could lose yourself for ever.[66]

The moral nature of the passivity he seeks is not so much complex as contradictory. 'A huge *graceless* wilderness where you could lose yourself forever' suggests limbo; but he would also seem to be attacking materialism as a faith from the standpoint of another faith and with truly religious fervour:

What he realized, and more clearly as time went on, was that money-worship has been elevated into a religion. Perhaps it is the only real religion – the only really *felt* religion – that is left to us. Money is what God used to be. Good and evil have no meaning any longer except failure and success. Hence the profoundly significant phrase, to *make good*. The decalogue has been reduced to two commandments. One for the employers – the elect, the money-priesthood as it were – 'Thou shalt make money'; the other for the employed – the slaves and underlings – 'Thou shalt not lose thy job'.[67]

Such a capitalist religion fails, it would seem, because of its fundamental denial of real relationship. So much of *Keep the Aspidistra Flying* is summed up in the adapted extract from Corinthians which serves as the book's epigraph:

Though I speak with the tongues of men and of angels, and have not money. I am become as a sounding brass, or a tinkling cymbal. And though I have the gift of prophesy, and understand all mysteries, and all knowledge; and though I have all faith, so that I could remove mountains, and have not money, I am nothing. And though I bestow all my goods to feed the poor, and though I give my body to be burned, and have not money, it profiteth me nothing. Money suffereth long, and is kind; money envieth not, money vaunteth not itself, is not puffed up, doth not

behave unseemly, seeketh not her own, is not easily pro-
voked, thinketh no evil; rejoiceth not in iniquity, but rejoiceth in the truth, beareth all things, believeth all things,
hopeth all things, endureth all things. . . . And now abideth
faith, hope, money, these three; but the greatest of these is
money.

The attack on the money-god is really an appeal for understanding and love and genuine community. Like Carlyle he
sees true relationship destroyed and replaced by what Carlyle
called the cash-nexus. Love is now dependent on money:

If you have no money, men won't care for you, women
won't love you; won't that is, care for you or love you the
least little bit that matters. And how right they are, after
all! For, moneyless, you are unlovable.[68]

In his heretical denunciation of the reigning faith, Comstock would seem to be asserting another: 'It was his religion,
you might say to keep out of that filthy money-world'.[69] And
so he withdraws to his equivalent of the anchorite's cave – a
slum room on the south bank, from which he could view the
world he had renounced with the contempt it deserved. But
what starts off as a fundamentalist repudiation of a corrupt
moral order, implying a brave continuation of the struggle to
keep pure and active the individual conscience, becomes passive submission. Beginning as an anchorite he becomes,
simply, a failure: one who has lost the battle and now wants
only to relinquish all responsibility for moral standards and
for the individual self. 'You don't seem to *want* to make any
effort', says Rosemary. 'You want to sink – just *sink*.' And
Comstock mentally agrees with her:

If only she would leave him alone! Alone, alone! Free from
the nagging consciousness of his failure; free to sink, as she
had said, down, down, into quiet worlds where money and
effort and moral obligation did not exist.[70]

That significant Orwellian word 'decency', meaning a personal secular and ultimately indefinable moral standard – a
sort of fiduciary issue not backed by God – crops up again, but
now, of course, only to be abandoned along with the struggle

of which it is symptomatic. We might recall Comstock's allusion to it in a passage quoted a few pages back:

> Before, he had fought against the money-code, and yet he had clung to his wretched remnant of decency. But now it was precisely from decency that he wanted to escape. He wanted to go down, deep down, into some world where decency no longer mattered; to cut the strings of his self-respect, to submerge himself − to *sink*, as Rosemary had said.[71]

In fact Orwell is a little disingenuous in his reliance on this word 'decency', for its roots are a lot less secular than the term itself seems to imply. Asking himself, in an article in *Time and Tide* (December 1940), what is the nature of Chaplin's peculiar gift, he concludes that it is the power to stand 'for the ineradicable belief in decency that exists in the hearts of ordinary people . . . everywhere, under the surface, the common man sticks obstinately to the beliefs that he derives from the Christian culture.'

At the very least, 'decency' acts as the symbol of integrity formerly provided by religion (to adopt a phrase of Erikson's). Orwell admits as much himself in a letter to Humphry House:

> . . . it is a good rule of thumb never to mention religion if you can possibly avoid it . . . In any case the churches no longer have any hold on the working class, except perhaps for the Catholic Irish labourers. On the other hand you can always appeal to common decency, which the vast majority of people believe in without the need to tie it up with any transcendental belief.[72]

G. K. Chesterton is supposed to have described Middleton Murry as 'the voice of one crying in the wilderness: "there is no God, and Marx is His prophet".' It is tempting to apply the comment to Orwell substituting 'decency' for Marx.

There is thus something more than a capricious play on words in Comstock's exchange with Ravelston over the latter's offer of help:

> 'But dash it all! You might as well have a decent place to

live in'.
'But I don't want a decent place. I want an indecent place.
This one, for instance'.[73]

In repudiating decency he is accepting that he now wants to
live morally beyond the pale – almost in the limbo of the
judged and the damned. This merging of the individual self in
the common identity of the sinner marks the end of his struggle to sustain that other personal identity. Comstock accepts –
with a characteristic touch of resentful self-pity – that he is
beaten, unable to match up to what was asked of him:

> At the bottom of all his feelings there was a sulkiness, a *je
> m'en fous* in the face of the world. Life had beaten him; but
> you can still beat life by turning your face away. Better to
> sink than rise. Down, down into the ghost-kingdom, the
> shadowy world where shame, effort, decency do not exist![74]

In fact this tenuous thread of self-pity continues to link him
with his previous moral world, and to carry his appeal for love
to its lost gods. Wallowing in what he can even refer to as 'the
ultimate mud' he convinces himself with a vengeful pleasure
that he is now too bad for anyone to want to save him:

> Surely *now* he was past redemption? Surely, try as they
> would, they couldn't prise him out of a hole like this? He
> had wanted to reach the mud – well, this was the mud,
> wasn't it?

There is the trace of a challenge in this and with it the sugges-
tion that he is not quite so irredeemably lost as he would have
us believe: that even in the 'ultimate mud' he knows very well
that some sort of salvation (and this is his word, too) remains
within earshot:

> That other world, the world of money and success, is
> always so strangely near. You don't escape it merely by
> taking refuse in dirt and misery . . . A letter, a telephone
> message, and from this squalor he could step straight back
> into the money-world – back to four quid a week, back to
> effort and decency and slavery. Going to the devil isn't so
> easy as it sounds. Sometimes your salvation hunts you
> down like the Hound of Heaven.[75]

So he is not – perhaps – past redemption after all; but what has he been saved *from* and *for*? Going to the devil means utter submissiveness and passivity: it means sinking down into that ghost kingdom where the only identity – equally available to all – is that of the sinner. Salvation, it seems, means coming back into the world again, accepting a role in it, and no longer disdaining the ruck of men, their preoccupations and their merits. Indeed it means renewed respect for the phenomenal world and for the *va-et-vient* of life where the humble are too busy living to spend time reflecting on the choice of life. A nascent sense of community begins to supplant his former isolation and alienation, the whole process recalling the experience of another central character in a book admired by Orwell:

> . . . with an almost audible click he felt the wheels of his being look up anew on the world without. Things that rode meaningless on the eyeball an instant before slid into proper proportion. Roads were meant to be walked upon, houses to be lived in, cattle to be driven, fields to be tilled, and men and women to be talked to. They were all real and true – solidly planted upon the feet – perfectly comprehensible – clay of his clay, neither more nor less.[76]

The comparison is close for in *Kim* Kipling is portraying a very similar identity-crisis, though for him the only alternative to identity through commitment is a terrifying moral disintegration.

Comstock, in his new-found regard for the treasure of the humble symbolised in the aspidistra still stops a little short of complete identification but his enthusiasm for their moral probity – to say nothing of his imminent fatherhood – shows how fully his faith has been reborn. It is faith once more in a world where decency, that personal moral standard, does exist, where people may live in the shadow of the money-god yet still retain their independence:

> He wondered about the people in houses like those. They would be, for example, small clerks, shop-assistants, commercial travellers, insurance touts, tram conductors. Did *they* know that they were only puppets dancing when money pulled the strings? You bet they didn't. And if they did,

what would they care? They were too busy being born, being married, begetting, working, dying. It mightn't be a bad thing, if you could manage it, to feel yourself one of them, one of the ruck of men. Our civilization is founded on greed and fear, but in the lives of common men the greed and fear are mysteriously transmuted into something nobler. The lower-middle-class people in there, behind their lace curtains, with their children and their scraps of furniture and their aspidistras – they lived by the money-code, sure enough, and yet they contrived to keep their decency. The money-code as they interpreted it was not merely cynical and hoggish. They had their standards, their inviolable points of honour. They 'kept themselves re-spectable' – kept the aspidistra flying. Besides, they were *alive*. They were bound up in the bundle of life. They begot children, which is what the saints and the soul-savers never by any chance do.

The aspidistra is the tree of life, he thought suddenly.[77]

Unfortunately this is not quite the whole story, for Orwell wants at the same time to suggest that Comstock's return is a self-betrayal. He commits himself to returning to the world by destroying his manuscript, the symbol and the product of his revolt:

He walked rapidly away. What had he done? Chucked up the sponge! Broken all his oaths! His long and lonely war had ended in ignominious defeat. Circumcise ye your fore-skins, saith the Lord. He was coming back to the fold, repentant.[78]

The confusion of allegiance is symptomised in the evocation of the image of the Prodigal Son: by returning to the fold he has, it appears, betrayed something – but what, precisely? From the quotation it looks as though it is his stand in the name of individualism, but there are objections to this. First-ly, he has *not* been conducting a 'long and lonely war' all the time. In that sort of war you concede defeat when you opt for the ghost-kingdom. The second objection is that what he has now done is to settle for a continuation of war, if not perhaps such a lonely one. 'Decency' and all that it implies is going to be sustained *in spite of* the money-god not because of him. In other words the morality of the puppets is not, simply, whatever is determined according to the money-code: they have their own peculiar (but by now rather familiar) freedom – the freedom to their own interpretation, by which they could keep themselves respectable according to their *own* code. Far from the battle being over, its ensign is to be seen in every window:

> The money-code as they interpreted it was not merely cynical and hoggish. They had their standards, their inviolable points of honour. They 'kept themselves respectable' – kept the aspidistra flying.

What he has certainly retreated from is his earlier fundamentalism when he refused to have any traffic whatsoever with the money-god, willing to cut all his ties if this was the only way to preserve himself and his faith unspotted. But the anchorite phase (the word is very much in Comstock's mind) is first and most fully betrayed by the succeeding phase of total resignation when he accepts that what he wants is not a decent place but an indecent one, in fact, a 'world where decency no longer mattered'.

The third phase – of reintegration – so emphatically labelled betrayal just does not earn such a description dramatically, and the chief reason is that there is not a big enough moral distinction between it and the first phase. Comstock has given up trying to reform the reformation but, as his admiration for the people behind the lace curtains reveals, he has not abandoned its fundamental ethic and so is still opposed to the orthodoxy of the money-code. Like Rasselas's hermit, he has decided that to secure himself from vice by retiring from the practice of virtue is no satisfactory solution; and like him he returns to the world.

Orwell's intention is, of course, all too clear. We are to see Comstock, doomed by his own inherent weakness and corruption, heading inexorably for the sands of spiritual destruction:

> His resolutions, now that he had broken them, seemed nothing but a frightful weight that he had cast off. Moreover, he was aware that he was only fulfilling his

destiny. In some corner of his mind he had always known that this would happen . . . For it was what, in his secret heart, he had desired.[79]

Considering what he is about to do, this is much too extravagant an indulgence in the language of confession and self-betrayal. It is like a voluntary and public unfrocking. Stripping himself of his moral self-sufficiency and indomitable will he admits that he is weakness and sin and that it is not possible for him to have an identity other than that of the sinner. But all that this does is to draw attention to the discrepancy between the tenor of the self-indictment and what it is that he is doing: the apostasy he surrenders to is nothing like as great as the language implies, and the abjectness of his capitulation is confessional over-kill. He is emphatically *not* surrendering his personal identity and accepting instead that of the sinner. After listening to the disclosure one is a little embarrassed to be reminded that all he yields to is the desire to get back into the world of 'decent' men:

> He wondered whether every anchorite in his dismal cell pines secretly to be back in the world of men. Perhaps there were a few who did not. Somebody or other had said that the modern world is only habitable by saints and scoundrels. He, Gordon, wasn't a saint. Better, then, to be an unpretending scoundrel along with the others. It was what he had secretly pined for; now that he had acknowledged his desire and surrendered to it, he was at peace.[80]

Despite the rhetoric, this is hardly enough to suggest that he has sold his soul. Yet there can be little doubt that such is the impression we are meant to get:

> He would be as though born anew. The sluttish poet of today would be hardly recognizable in the natty young business man of tomorrow. They would take him back, right enough; he had the talent they needed. He would buckle to work, sell his soul, and hold down his job.[81]

The attempted irony just does not work: not only because the sell-out is not really a sell-out — decency is still an objective, and struggle and effort are implied in accepting it as such —

but also because Comstock *is*, in a sense, born anew in his rediscovery of the warmth and humanity of those lower-middle-class people behind their lace curtains who were not saints but who had learned how to live. Moreover, there are too many devils. If 'going to the devil' means, as it is affirmed earlier, surrendering to utter passivity, then it can't also mean joining the aspidistra-set.

It might just conceivably be objected that we are meant to see Comstock as admitting defeat too soon, subsequently coming to realise that he has not lost his soul but gained it. But if this is the case, all the fuss at the end about surrender, about honestly facing up to unpalatable truths, about always knowing that this would happen, is self-indulgent humbug. Moreover he continues to talk of surrender till the final moment when he drops *London Pleasures*, the symbol of his uncompromising, anchorite individualism, into the sewer – no doubt to be chewed up by a pack of Orwellian rats:

> He unrolled a page of *London Pleasures*. In the middle of the labyrinthine scrawlings a line caught his eye. Momentary regret stabbed him. After all, parts of it weren't half bad! If only it could ever be finished! It seemed such a shame to shy it away after all the work he had done on it. Save it, perhaps? Keep it by him and finish it secretly in his spare time? Even now it might come to something.
> No, no! Keep your parole. Either surrender or don't surrender.
> He doubled up the manuscript and stuffed it between the bars of the drain. It fell with a plop into the water below.
> *Vicisti, O aspidistra!*[82]

It would appear that he has conceded defeat in his efforts to sustain complete personal independence. But it is equally clear that the aspidistra has conquered not because of his own spiritual and moral flaccidity but because it offers an alternative objective which is very far indeed from being morally despicable, and which encourages a response very far from passive.

Keep the Aspidistra Flying is clearly not a success and the reason could well be identified as a massive failure in irony. And here this is as much a moral as an aesthetic failure. Irony as a literary mode is grounded in opposition and antithesis and requires above all toughness of discrimination and firmness of moral vision: which amounts to a catalogue of this novel's deficiences.

When Comstock complains that going to the devil isn't as easy as it sounds, salvation hunting you down like the Hound of Heaven, we accept it coming from him as an irony: salvation by and for the money-god. In the end, however, he is indeed saved for 'the world', and the book concludes with the pious optimism of Comstock on his knees listening for the sound of the unborn child:

> For a long time he remained kneeling there, his head pressed against the softness of her belly. She clasped her hands behind his head and pulled it closer. He could hear nothing, only the blood drumming in his own ear. But she could not have been mistaken. Somewhere in there, in the safe, warm, cushioned darkness, it was alive and stirring. Well, once again things were happening in the Comstock family.[83]

So for all his other references to returning to the world and embracing the aspidistra:

> He looked back over the last two frightful years. He had blasphemed against money, rebelled against money, tried to live like an anchorite outside the money-world; and it had brought him not only misery, but also a frightful emptiness, an inescapable sense of futility. To abjure money is to abjure life. Be not righteous over much; why shouldst thou die before thy time?[84]

The irony cannot work because the alternatives presented are not genuine moral opposites.

Shadowed in behind the inadequate tension of the pseudo-antithesis of eremetic individualism and social self-commitment, there is a third moral position amounting to a genuine, if only nascent, antithesis to each of the others. This is the complete self-abnegation epitomised in Comstock's deep desire to escape 'from all effort and all decency'. It is undoubtedly a moment of surrender and submission, when Comstock dwells on his spiritual vacuity with grateful satisfaction. There is real self-betrayal here much more profound than the alleged betrayal which excites so much verbal flagellation later in the book. But Orwell has decided that, despite the powerful appeal from this quarter, Comstock must not end here in this (genuine) degradation but should return to the world he has earlier repudiated and end with considerable fuss about a much more equivocal degradation. As it stands, the ending tends to rewrite Comstock's spiritual progress leaving the language of confession and betrayal hanging in the air, lacking assimilation, but curiously persistent and active in its own interest.

The polarity making its shadowy and confused appearance here is of a combative individualism (Comstock's earlier position, and, arguably, the one he is returning to since it is the people who impress him with their independence who prompt his decision), and a total passivity – a total surrender of individuality and the cause of individualism. When this is projected a little further, and more uncompromisingly with self-deceiving individualism facing up to its inadequacies and conceding its *desire* for what is the absolutist solution, the language of confession and betrayal comes into its own. The achievement of *Nineteen Eighty-Four* is precisely in this: that here, in his last book, Orwell for the first time fully and brilliantly assimilates this tension to his creative effort. Openly acknowledged and unambiguous, it no longer lurks neurotically in dark corners exhibiting itself furtively and incompletely here and there, but offers itself instead as a coherent and self-consistent vision of man's relationship to himself and his world. It is only in *Nineteen Eighty-Four* that this writer so celebrated for his honesty seems to me to be really honest, for this novel is the true expression of what Dan Jacobson has described as 'the confrontation between a man and the necessities of his own nature, out of which all first-class work springs.'[85]

It is now obvious why it is worth giving so much attention to the unsatisfactory ending of a thoroughly mediocre novel. In it we can see the continuation of a theme and the clear anticipation of future development. Guilt, heresy, and self-betrayal ultimately so well integrated in the appropriate fictive paradigm of *Nineteen Eighty-Four*, sticks out here in palpably unassimilated fragments.

5 The Sigh of the Soul

Religion is the sigh of the soul in a soulless world.

Karl Marx

O Lord I believe. Help thou my unbelief.

St Mark

The promise is only a promise, the fabulous
Country impartially far.

W.H. Auden

So far, Orwell has been shown to be the quite conscious inheritor of a specific religious tradition. In it he saw the orgin of
that liberal-christian culture to which the doctrine of the personal self was fundamental. But no more fundamental than it
was to Orwell himself; which is the reason for the religious passion that he brought to its defence. From it he drew a morality
and an identity, together with a purpose which sent him forth
with a mission to bettle for man's soul in the face of encroaching
darkness. By now, of course, we are also aware that he was
fighting his battle on two fronts; there being an internal one as
well as an external.

It should be obvious, too, by this time that to use the terminology of religious faith is not to conjure words out of the
air. The vocabulary is instinctively Orwell's own and his particular use of it offers further insight into the nature of his
personal problem. Disbelieving in God, he believes in the
personal soul; though by and large he substitutes 'self' for
'soul'. The latter word is, nevertheless, frequently preferred
and his recipe for sustaining the self is a straight adaption of
a familiar methodology for a more explicitly spiritual salvation – namely, strict adherence to the classical Puritan virtues and submission to the creed's traditional requirements.
In seeking this salvation for himself and others he describes

with remarkable fidelity the temper as well as the tactics of the archetypal Puritan hero. Even in his battle with himself when he was strongly tempted to lay down his arms and purge his individualist heresy he was behaving in a way by no means foreign to his tradition.

To link the terminology he instinctively uses with the intensity and fidelity of his defence of the creed, is at once to become sceptical about any account which holds that Orwell regarded religion simply as social glue. If we go further and compare him with some writers who did regard belief in this light the discrepancy between their ethic and his becomes immediately obvious. There is, for example none of the emphasis on solidarity and community that is found in Conrad. Orwell would never be the begetter of such an expression as 'Woe to the stragglers! We exist only insofar as we hang together'. He could never have invented a Brierly who kills himself when the code of the Merchant Marine by which he had lived is desecrated by one of its members. He would certainly never have used as an epigraph to one of his novels, as Conrad did, Novalis's dictum: 'It is certain any conviction gains infinitely the moment another soul will believe in it'.

Nor is there, in Orwell, anything of the intense almost psychotic fear of isolation that we find in Kipling who was prepared to sacrifice so much in order to secure a sense of his own individual existence. He could never have written the short story 'Beyond the Pale' where after recounting how a young Indian girl suffers dreadful mutilation as a punishment for allowing an Englishman to woo her, Kipling can draw the moral that it is fundamentally wrong – not to hack off a girl's limbs, but to cross the frontiers between East and West: to cross any frontiers in fact, for they are there to give shape and 'reality' to our existence. Nor is there any tendency in Orwell to see chaos as reality and himself impelled to bend all his efforts to establish and maintain a nice economy of self in the midst of it. There could never be for him the fine profit and loss accounting that goes on in Kipling, summed up in the quotation on page 27.

For Orwell the essential question is something quite different. To him belief is not an existential aid, save in the sense in which it might be considered so by a Christian; it was not primarily a structural device, but a spiritual necessity. Certainly nothing could be further from the truth than Rieff's claim that Orwell is so completely outside religious experience as 'to conceive of religion as most basically a mode of social cohesion'. He is not asking how to build a world but how to build a *moral* world; and, given the sort of world he sees as moral the next question must be, how do you make an individual if there is no soul. The difference between him and the man Rieff describes is the difference between the *homo religiosus* and the existentialist.

The purpose of this chapter is to offer further and more specific evidence against the view that for Orwell the death of religious belief was the *fait accompli* it might at first glance seem to be. Not only is there proof that a battle of belief is still being fought out in his work, but a good deal of the evidence is to be found in a very significant quarter; namely, his ferocious attacks on *other* religious systems. In other words there is also a battle of beliefs.

That religious belief is on the decline is, of course, not questioned by Orwell but it is as much the spiritual as the social consequences which are of immediate concern to him:

> For two hundred years we had sawed and sawed and sawed at the branch we were sitting on. And in the end, much more suddenly than anyone had foreseen, our efforts were rewarded, and down we came. But unfortunately there had been a little mistake. The thing at the bottom was not a bed of roses after all, it was a cesspool full of barbed wire.

The point is that we *were* sitting on the branch: where are we to sit now? This is the question that haunts virtually all of Orwell's work, not in the crudely existential sense of how to get by, after the manner of Kipling or Conrad, but as a problem which is fundamentally teleological. 'The basic problem of our time is the decay of belief in personal immortality', he had written,

> and it seems it cannot be dealt with while the average human being is either drudging like an ox or shivering in fear of the secret police.[2]

However it remains the major problem, and we are not to

assume 'like most Socialists' that 'all problems lapse when one's belly is full':

> . . . the truth is the opposite: when one's belly is empty, one's only problem is an empty belly. It is when we have got away from drudgery and exploitation that we shall really start wondering about man's destiny and the reason for his existence.[3]

It is significant that the loss of religious belief conveys itself to Orwell most immediately in terms not of a loss of contact with God but of a lost confidence in personal immortality. On his own account this would place him firmly in the Christian tradition:

> Western civilisation, unlike some oriental civilisations, was founded partly on the belief in individual immortality. If one looks at the Christian religion from outside, this belief appears far more important than the belief in God.[4]

And more and more he comes to concern himself with the notion of individual immortality – of the 'personal soul' – as his belief in the personal self begins to waver under the relentless pressure to which it has always been subjected. Can his particular concept of the personal self, so much more than a Kiplingesque scissors-and-paste job, really survive if the notion of soul has to be abandoned? And what will replace it if it doesn't? These are the questions which raise profound anxiety in Orwell. In a review of F. J. Sheed's book *Communism and Man*, he wrote:

> As he sees clearly enough, the radical difference between Christian and Communist lies in the question of personal immortality. Either this life is a preparation for another, in which case the individual soul is all-important, or there is no life after death, in which case the individual is merely a replaceable cell in the general body.[5]

The individual then will have no personal spiritual significance of his own. Such observations quite clearly associate the idea of personal self with that of the individual soul, as he calls it. The term might be secularised – though it is a term he seemingly can't avoid – but he needs and embraces its moral and religious dimensions all the same. For Orwell is emphatically not concerned with personal self simply as existential form. For him, by an identification of soul and personal self, the individual is possessed of a moral sense and the means to establish for himself a moral system whereby good and evil can clearly be distinguished. This is the integrity which Orwell initially laid claim to: but it was one where the components were mutually dependent. Destroy a man's moral system, confuse his moral sense and his individuality was destroyed too. Winston Smith we might recall, was quite unable to rouse Julia to the significance of his daily forgeries in the Records Department:

> Such things did not appear to horrify her. She did not feel the abyss opening beneath her feet at the thought of lies becoming truths.[6]

Attack from the other side by repudiating the notion of soul, and the problem of defining a personal morality was rendered insurmountable, in turn proving the concept of the personal self hollow (if it could not act effectively without the moral support of soul).

It is entirely compatible with Orwell's Protestant background firstly that he should attach such significance to the 'individual' soul and secondly that the major question for him should then be how to establish a morality without this inner light. 'The basic problem of our time is the decay of belief in personal immortality', he had said and a later variant he gives it makes the latent connection explicit:

> The real problem of our time is to restore the sense of absolute right and wrong when the belief it used to rest on – that is, the belief in personal immortality – has been destroyed. This demands faith which is a different thing from credulity.[7]

The frequency with which he returns to the point suggests just how important the moral issue was to him. The 'western concept of good and evil is very difficult to separate from [the belief in individual immortality]'; yet, things being as they are, man has to make the effort to 'evolve a system of good and evil which is independent of heaven and hell'.[8]

Orwell is continuously seeking such a 'system'; forever urging us – and perhaps himself – to face up to the fact that the old one had gone and that ours is the responsibility for finding another to put in its place:

> I do not want the belief in life after death to return, and in any case it is not likely to return. What I do point out is that its disappearance has left a big hole, and that we ought to take notice of the fact.

And he adds:

> One cannot have any worthwhile picture of the future unless one realises how much we have lost by the decay of Christianity.[9]

Any tendency to ignore the existence of the hole is denounced with all the fervour an archetypal Protestant might bring to the sinner who neither saw the perilous state he was in, nor acknowledged his prime responsibility to seek his own salvation, The Roman Catholic intelligentsia are, it seems, notoriously culpable in this respect. In sniggering at 'anyone simple enough to suppose that the Fathers of the Church meant what they said' they are merely 'raising smoke-screens to conceal their own disbelief from themselves'.[10] Not that he is primarily worried about their spiritual welfare: only, in laying their smoke-screen 'a vitally important fact – that one of the props of western civilisation has been knocked away – is obscured'.[11]

The comparison with the Protestants is again a fair one for the hole that Orwell is so conscious of, is, if one may put it like this, a Protestant one. Without belief in the individual soul (it is characteristic of Orwell that he should include the adjective), confidence in one's right and ability to reason and so to *choose* for oneself – to make moral distinctions – is fatally eroded and one's moral sense exposed to confusion. All one can do then is accept, and abandon the achievement so delicately described in one of Auden's poems:

> . . . finally, there came a childish creature
> On whom the years could model any feature,
> Fake, as chance fell, a leopard or a dove.
>
> Who by the gentlest wind was rudely shaken,

Who looked for truth but always was mistaken,
And envied his few friends, and chose his love.

Faith vanishes, then, but, as the kindred temper of Dorothy Hare in *A Clergyman's Daughter* conceded, the need for faith remains. But faith in what, and how could it be sustained when there is no fixed point, no absolute, to offer it anchorage? Such faith would indeed be 'a very different thing from credulity'.

In fact it is impossible for him because ultimately he cannot see faith as separable from soul. Again his situation recalls that of Dorothy Hare:

> Beliefs change, thoughts change, but there is some inner part of the soul that does not change. Faith vanishes, but the need for faith remains the same as before.[12]

Like Dorothy he disbelieves in God but much more than her he remains true to the notion of soul. Of course he will only admit the term in a metaphorical sense, but he seems to find it difficult to think of soul as being truly a metaphor for anything; so strong is his sense of its moral reality. Nevertheless the concept of soul comes to seem to him as much a cultural idea as the concept of the personal self:

> Reared for thousands of years on the notion that the individual survives, man has got to make a considerable psychological effort to get used to the notion that the individual perishes.[13]

This was written in 1944. Yet though the tone sounds firm and businesslike and the conclusion cut-and-dried it is followed by no convincing sign that this diet of rationalism is capable of assuaging the hunger for some other solution.

A few pages back I quoted a passage from one of Orwell's articles which described how modern man had succeeded in sawing off the branch he was sitting on and had landed in a cess- pool full of barbed wire. The extract comes from a piece Orwell contributed to *Time and Tide* in 1940 with the title of 'Notes on the Way'. It is worth looking at in some detail since it supplies a full, if confused, picture of the perceptions, doubts and desires which attended Orwell's self-questioning on the subject of belief.

He begins by describing the 'rather cruel trick' he played on
the wasp, he cut in half. The occasion has already been
referred to but its relevance here merits a closer look.

> He was sucking jam on my plate, and I cut him in half. He
> paid no attention, merely went on with his meal, while a
> tiny stream of jam trickled out of his severed oesophagus.
> Only when he tried to fly away did he grasp the dreadful
> thing that had happened to him.[14]

In various ways the experiment and his close observation of it
are highly typical of Orwell. Then he proceeds in the best
Lutheran tradition to draw from his observation a moral:

> It is the same with modern man. The thing that has been
> cut away is his soul, and there was a period – twenty years,
> perhaps – during which he did not notice it.

To think in this way is itself to suggest the temper of the *homo
religiosus* despite the brisk repudiation of the next sentence: 'It
was absolutely necessary that the soul should be cut away'.
Our suspicion that the vigour of the language is not quite the
token of unambiguous approval for the quick, clean kill that it
seems to be, is substantiated as the article goes on. The
metaphor changes and the mutilation of the wasp becomes *felo
de se*. We, presumably mistakenly, succeeded in sawing
through the branch on which we were sitting. Well, if not mistakenly at least with inadequate forethought:

> But unfortunately there had been a little mistake. The thing
> at the bottom was not a bed of roses but a cesspool full of
> barbed wire.

Religious belief – here identified with the soul – cannot then
be cursorily dismissed after all. It may have come to be 'in essence a lie, a semi-conscious device for keeping the rich rich
and the poor poor', but without it man's moral nature could
not sustain itself: the good it seems would be all too easily
interred with its bones, leaving evil to triumph:

> . . . if one assumes that no sanction can ever be effective
> except the supernatural one, it is clear what follows. There
> is no wisdom except in the fear of God; but nobody fears

God; therefore there is no wisdom. Man's history reduces itself to the rise and fall of material civilisation, one Tower of Babel after another. In that case we can be pretty certain what is ahead of us. Wars and yet more wars, revolutions and counter-revolutions, Hitlers and super-Hitlers – and so downward into abysses which are horrible to contemplate.

Which returns us to the impasse:

So it appears that amputation of the soul *isn't* just a simple surgical job, like having your appendix out. The wound has a tendency to go septic.

Though we may detect a bias, precisely where Orwell stands in all this is by no means clear: but it is just this ambivalence which has placed him in the spiritual cleft-stick described in the foregoing pages. And there is much more in the same vein: reservation upon reservation. Religion we notice is not thrown out, bell, book and candle, so to speak; it is 'Religious belief, *in the form we had known it.*' which had to be abandoned. And it is not God but the 'God of the Prayer Book' who (still a trifle speculatively) no longer exists. Nor does he say that the amputation of the soul is not a simple surgical job: it *appears* that it is not.

Saw off the branch, depose Christianity but – 'had Zimri peace, who slew his master?' Orwell demonstrates in so many ways how little peace was available to him now that the liberal – Christian era had lost its guarantor. He detects and describes with palpable fellow-feeling the reflection of his own ambivalence in the quandary of other writers:

What you do feel all through [*Ulysses*], however, is the conviction from which Joyce cannot escape, that the whole of this modern world which he is describing has no meaning in it now that the teachings of the Church are no longer credible. He is yearning after the religious faith which the two or three generations preceding him had had to fight against in the name of religious liberty.[15]

Sometimes his reconstruction of the others' position comes near to being a definitive summary of his own. Baudelaire, for example,

clung to the ethical and imaginative background of Christianity, because he had been brought up in the Christian
tradition and because he perceived that such notions as sin,
damnation, etc. were in a sense truer and more real than
anything he could get from sloppy, humanitarian atheism.
Spiritually the Christian cosmos suited him, though as a
rule he preferred to turn it upside down. But, of course, he
was not and could not make himself a believer in the same
literal sense as the people who go to church on Sunday; so it
was natural that he should sometimes attack Christian
ethics from without instead of from within.

It is perhaps a rather complicated attitude, but natural
enough at a time when religious belief was decaying. . . .[16]

What emerges from Orwell's forebodings, reservations and
nostalgia offers concrete evidence of his inability to bring
order to his spiritual disorientation; and there is both bewilder-
ment and urgency – and also, perhaps, a suppressed anguish –
in his pleading:

The Kingdom of Heaven has somehow got to be brought on
to the surface of the earth. We have got to be the children of
God, even though the God of the Prayer Book no longer
exists.[17]

The first sentence could be, and to a degree is, a reiteration of
the Puritan's desire 'to crystallise a moral ideal in the daily life
of a visible society' as Tawney put: but the second reveals the
writer as a Puritan whose tenuous link with the God of the
Prayer Book has snapped and who is now desperately trying
to save himself from drifting off from all moral conviction. It is
an appeal to the religious consciousness but once again
without an absolute for it to focus upon, as the borrowed terminology makes clear. J.S. Whale in *The Protestant Tradition*
describes Orwell's predicament succinctly when he argues
that liberalism without a world-transcending faith is 'wistful
and lost':

It complains that a Hitler, a Stalin or any dictator typical of
the modern age has no sense of the sanctity of individual
personality. This is true. It is the most ghastly truth of our

time. But if there be no living God, the sovereign Creator and Redeemer in whose image man is made, why should the individual take precedence over the mass; over Party or Nation or Race? Why should the ant be more important than the ant-heap? Take away faith in the living God who made man for himself, and who overarches the whole human scene in his transcendent sovereignty – and the special status of the individual is gone. That place of honour which liberal philosophy claims for him is his only because Christ died for him. [18]

In setting out to confront the reality of the absent soul Orwell has shown his own incapacity to accept this absence fully and finally as non-existence, or to give up his search for a system which would satisfactorily incorporate it. The 'real problem' is still how to 'restore the religious attitude while accepting death as final'. [19] However, in the middle of the article just discussed he gives a remarkable and unexpected emphasis to an urge in man which opens the prospect of a quite different solution, and one that would not only supply soul – with a distinctly pre-Lutheran form – but a church to go with it:

> Man is not an individual, he is only a cell in an everlasting body and he is dimly aware of it. There is no other way of explaining why it is that men will die in battle. It is nonsense to say that they only do it because they are driven . . . Men die in battle – not gladly, of course, but at any rate voluntarily – because of abstractions called 'honour', 'duty', 'patriotism' and so forth.
>
> All that this really means is that they are aware of some organism greater than themselves, stretching into the future and the past, within which they feel themselves to be immortal.

That 'all' is a little breath-taking, for what it describes is self-abnegation in the mystic language of transcendental idealism; followed by a disarming confession of an identikit divinity which holds all together:

> 'Who dies if England live?' sounds like a piece of bombast, but if you alter 'England' to whatever you prefer, you can

see that it expresses one of the main motives of human conduct.[20]

Unsurprisingly, he concludes that man does not live by bread alone, but by adherence to a personal ideal which, it would appear, is itself somehow a facet of a larger communal idealism transcending the individual.

It hardly seems that this is what is meant by establishing the Kingdom of Heaven on the surface of the earth. What the passage does show, however, is the alternative direction Orwell veers towards when his confidence in the nexus of 'individual' soul and personal self is exhausted. As we have seen, the tendency has been there from the beginning, and not least in the peculiar form taken by his ambiguous antagonism to totalitarianism. In *Nineteen Eighty-Four*, as we shall see, it achieves its full apotheosis.

That Orwell is what might be described as organically opposed to totalitarianism has already been established. It seemed to him to be fundamentally inimical to any cultural and moral integrity based on the notion of the personal self. What is specially interesting, however, is that totalitarianism increasingly takes on the colouring of an alternative, *confessional* system.

At first his linking together of the Communist Party and the Roman Catholic Church seems little more than analogical convenience: the Communist Party in its heresy-trials and inquisitorial methods recalling the Church in its absolutist hey-day. Even then it is often the Roman Catholics who bear the full brunt of his ferocious attacks; a fact which cannot be satisfactorily accounted for either by regarding them as a stalking-horse for Communist Party totalitarianism or by reference to the literary antagonisms of the inter-war years when Catholics formed an identifiable literary 'party'. Comparisons between them are so insistent and distinctions so often blurred that, morally, the Communist Party begins to look like the Catholic Church in mufti and the Catholic Church – to adapt a well-known adage – like the Communist Party on its knees. The explanation is, of course, that it is not simply totalitarianism but a *confessional* totalitarianism which poses the greatest threat to Orwell's fluctuating confidence in the idea of the personal self; and the greatest attraction.

Certainly due weight must be given to literary animosities of the period where writers did tend to commit themselves to one or other of the prevailing ideologies. It may be remembered that Orwell himself had recommended such commitment as the only way out of 'the consciousness of futility'[21] but he was at the same time highly suspicious of any attempt to foist orthodoxy upon him. Looking back from the vantage point of 1942, his summary of 'the successive literary cliques' who polarised artistic faith was not a flattering one:

> The life of a clique is about five years and I have been writing long enough to see three of them come and two go – the Catholic gang, the Stalinist gang, and the present pacifist or, as they are sometimes nicknamed, Fascist gang. My case against all of them is that they write mentally dishonest propaganda and degrade literary criticism to mutual arse-licking.[22]

The issue is not, however, basically one of literary fashion: what Orwell is again describing is the individual very much alone in the middle of a battle, his spiritual freedom fought over by totalitarian gangs – or simply totalitarianism. The image thus projected bears a marked similarity to that visualised for Charles Dickens in the closing sentence of his essay on the novelist. There 'the face behind the page' is, for Orwell,

> . . . the face of a man who is always fighting against something, but who fights in the open and is not frightened, the face of a man who is *generously angry* – in other words, of a nineteenth-century liberal, a free intelligence, a type hated with equal hatred by all the smelly little orthodoxies which are now contending for our souls.[23]

The connection is obvious. This is the image of Protestant individualism, very influential in the 19th century, still active in the 20th: it is man as Orwell wished, and, with a large part of his being felt him to be. But the 'smelly little orthodoxies' will not be so easily dismissed and to refer to them as he does here is to indulge in a little whistling in the dark. Behind these variants, as he well knows, is the coalescent form of Orthodoxy itself, implacably opposed to the heretic – whether his heresy was 'political, moral, religious or aesthetic' – whom '*the Protestant centuries*' (my italics) had defined as 'one who refused to outrage his own conscience'.

In challenging the old Orthodoxy, the Protestant revolution had in Orwell's eyes, equated the idea of intellectual integrity with the idea of rebellion, establishing the free individual conscience in the process. Now, it is precisely the achievement of these Protestant centuries which is threatened by a new Orthodoxy, and not surprisingly Orwell quite deliberately blurs the distinctions between the new and the old.

What, perhaps, is more surprising however, is that he does not stop there, but goes on to invest the new Orthodoxy with the religious colour and function of the earlier, making it appear as appealing to, and operating upon, the confessional instinct of man rather than anything more material.

So, to repeat, the constant comparisons with the Roman Catholic Church are anything but loosely analogical. Not that the Communist and the Catholic are saying the same thing – 'in a sense they are even saying opposite things': yet 'from the point of view of an outsider they are very much alike':

> If you want to find a book as evil-spirited as [Mirsky's] *The Intelligentsia of Great Britain*, the likeliest place to look is among the popular Roman Catholic apologists. You will find there the same venom and the same dishonesty, though, to do the Catholic justice, you will not usually find the same bad manners. Queer that Comrade Mirsky's spiritual brother should be Father – –![24]

As might be expected from the still-empiricist Orwell, it is in intellectual circles that the resemblance between Communist and Catholic is most pointed: it is the intellectual above all others who stands for the completest orthodoxy:

> One of the analogies between Communism and Roman Catholicism is that only the 'educated' are completely orthodox . . . the really interesting thing about [Catholic converts]* is the way in which they have worked out the supposed implications of orthodoxy until the tiniest details

* Orwell is here drawing a contrast between 'real Catholics' and converts: 'Ronald Knox. Arnold Lunn *et hoc genus*'.

of life are involved. Even the liquids you drink, apparently, can be orthodox or heretical; hence the campaigns of Chesterton, 'Beachcomber', etc., against tea and in favour of beer. According to Chesterton, tea-drinking is 'pagan', while beer-drinking is 'Christian' and coffee is 'the Puritan's opium'.[25]

It has been suggested already that Orwell not only distrusted but feared the intellectual and the explanation offered then is endorsed here. Once again Orwell's own moral position is being undermined by them; for the disturbing thing about their whole-hearted support of orthodoxy is that they are merely carrying to a logical extreme the individual's need, which Orwell profoundly realised, for a faith:

> . . . what do you achieve, after all, by getting rid of such primal things as patriotism and religion? You have not necessarily got rid of the need for *something to believe in*. There had been a sort of false dawn a few years earlier when numbers of young intellectuals, including several quite gifted writers . . . had fled into the Catholic Church. It is significant that these people went almost invariably to the Roman Church and not, for instance, to the C of E, the Greek Church or the Protestant sects. They went, that is, to the church with a world-wide organisation, the one with a rigid discipline, the one with power and prestige behind it. . . . I do not think one needs to look further than this for the reason why the young writers of the 'thirties flocked into or towards the Communist Party. It was simply something to believe in. Here was a church, an army, an orthodoxy, a discipline. Here was a Fatherland and – at any rate since 1935 or thereabouts – a Fuehrer. All the loyalties and superstitions that the intellect had seemingly banished could come rushing back under the thinnest of disguises. Patriotism, religion, empire, military glory – all in one word, Russia. Father, King, leader, hero, saviour – all in one word, Stalin. God – Stalin. The devil – Hitler. Heaven – Moscow. Hell – Berlin. All the gaps were filled up. So, after all, the 'Communism' of the English intellectual is something explicable enough. It is the patriotism of the deracinated.[26]

And, it would seem, the religion of the unbeliever. The scheme
set out here in 'Inside the Whale' (1940) is an interesting one
and ought to be held in mind when we come to discuss *Nineteen
Eighty-Four*, by which time the space to be occupied in it by
Winston Smith will be clearly predictable.

In 'Notes on Nationalism' (1945) he returns to the theme:

> Among the intelligentsia, it hardly needs saying that the
> dominant form of nationalism is Communism . . . A Com-
> munist, for my purpose here, is one who looks upon the
> USSR as his Fatherland and feels it his duty to justify Rus-
> sian policy and advance Russian interests at all costs . . .
>
> Ten or twenty years ago, the form of nationalism most
> closely corresponding to Communism today was political
> Catholicism.[27]

In 1946 he is drawing the same analogy:

> Fifteen years ago, when one defended the freedom of the
> intellect, one had to defend it against Conservatives, against
> Catholics, and to some extent . . . against Fascists. Today
> one has to defend it against Communists and 'fellow-
> travellers'.[28]

But if the intelligentsia were weak enough to allow its need for
something to believe in to lead it into honouring false gods, this
does not alter the capacity of Orthodoxy in either shape not
only to exert fascination but to satisfy these people's longings
and provide them with a theology. Both Communist Party
and Catholic Church, of course, are absolutist in claiming personal possession of the ark of the covenant:

> . . . each of them tacitly claims that the 'truth' has already
> been revealed, and that the heretic, if he is not simply a fool,
> is secretly aware of 'the truth' and merely resists it out of
> selfish motives.[29]

But Orwell repeatedly draws attention also to their similarity
in ecclesiastical structure. We see this very clearly in *Nineteen
Eighty-Four* but the version of Party organisation we get there,
has been anticipated many times before in direct comment. In
'The Prevention of Literature', for example, we are told that

'A totalitarian state is in effect a theocracy, and its ruling caste, in order to keep its position, has to be thought of as infallible'.[30] And in a review of Eliot's *Notes Towards the Definition of Culture* he describes how the Russian Communist Party could give itself stability and durability and become an eternal church comparable to the Church of Rome:

> Hereditary institutions . . . have the virtue of being unstable. They must be so, because power is constantly devolving upon people who are either incapable of holding it, or use it for purposes not intended by their forefathers. It is impossible to imagine any hereditary body lasting so long, and with so little change, as an adoptive organisation like the Catholic Church. And it is at least thinkable that another adoptive and authoritarian organisation, the Russian Communist Party, will have a similar history . . . if it continues to co-opt its members from all strata of society, and then train them into the desired mentality, it might keep its shape almost unaltered from generation to generation. In aristocratic societies the eccentric aristocrat is a familiar figure, but the eccentric commissar is almost a contradiction in terms.[31]

What the blurring of distinctions between Communist Party and Catholic Church signifies is now clearer. Totalitarian orthodoxy is a continuous and ever-present threat which Orwell like the watchful Puritan he is, and armed cap-à-pie, stands ready to rebut. The 'ism' may change but the character of the assault and the objective are the same. So he can pursue his undiscriminating attacks upon 'smelly little orthodoxies' with old-style fundamentalist vigour precisely because the battle lines are the same. What 'they' are after and what he is defending is his soul.

Naturally, then, the vocabulary of the two ideologies is made readily inter-changeable and in being so, affirms a relationship which is organic rather than analogical. When we are told that 'what we are moving towards at the moment is something more like the Spanish Inquisition'[32], the sense is literal rather than metaphoric. This is the context in which we have to see his invective against 'stinking' Roman Catholics[33], slightly excessive if it were prompted simply by literary animosity.

Not that Orwell regards Roman Catholicism as entirely a spent force: either that or else in blurring distinctions, he has confused himself. At any rate there are times when he talks as if the Counter-Reformation has yet to come. His tongue *may* be in his cheek in this letter to a friend:

> Have you ever looked into the window of one of those Bible Society Shops? I did today and saw huge notices 'The cheapest Roman Catholic Bible 5/6d. The cheapest Protestant Bible 1/-, The Douay version *not* stocked here', etc., etc. Long may they fight, I say: so long as that spirit is in the land we are safe from the RCs. . . .[34]

– it may be, but it is certainly not in 'Toward European Unity' where the authoritarian Catholic Church is seen to be as subtle and as powerful an enemy to genuine Socialism as the Party itself:

> As the struggle between East and West becomes more naked, there is danger that democratic Socialists and mere reactionaries will be driven into combining in a sort of Popular Front. The Church is the likeliest bridge between them. In any case the Church will make every effort to capture and sterilise any movement aiming at European unity. The dangerous thing about the Church is that it is *not* reactionary in the ordinary sense. It is not tied to *laissez-faire* or to the existing class system, and will not necessarily perish with them. It is perfectly capable of coming to terms with Socialism, or appearing to do so, provided that its own position is safeguarded. But if it is allowed to survive as a powerful organisation, it will make the establishment of true Socialism impossible, because its influence is and always must be against freedom of thought and speech, against human equality, and against any form of society tending to promote earthly happiness.[35]

We have, however, only to think of *Nineteen Eighty-Four* at this point to realise the fluidity of boundaries between the two totalitarian ideologies. Casting the Catholic Church as one of the seriously contending orthodoxies serves primarily to underline the confessional aspect of the totalitarianism most feared by Orwell.

In 'Why I write' (1946) Orwell admits that not even by the end of 1935 had he reached 'a firm decision' about his political – in the widest sense of that word – commitment; and he quotes a poem he wrote at the time 'expressing my dilemma'. It describes two forces contending for his soul while he walks like a guilty man between them:

> I am the worm who never turned
> The eunuch without a harem,
> Between the priest and commissar
> I walk like Eugene Aram;[36]

Even in 1935 the polarity of individual 'soul' – possibly a guilty one at that if we are to take the allusion to Eugene Aram seriously – and totalitarian orthodoxies is established. As time goes on the two orthodoxies merge into one, gradually defining confessional totalitarianism as the main threat – or principal attraction – to the personal self. Some fourteen years after Orwell wrote the poem, the opposing tensions described in the excerpt are resolved beyond question by the appearance of that priestly commissar O'Brien in the dominant role of inquisitorial deliverer.

It is towards the second pole that Orwell shows the twentieth-century inheritor of the Protestant tradition to be irresistibly drawn. With his faith in the personal self and the 'individual soul' waning or extinguished, the need for faith survives to seek fulfilment in some larger body. The intelligentsia in their determination to find something to believe in, had 'gone over', thus earning Orwell's extreme displeasure. Yet it is clear from an analysis of Orwell's moral vision that he was himself spiritually and morally inclined in the same direction; and the suspicion grows that he denounces the defecting intellectual so ferociously because he perceives in him his own latent self-betrayal. It is the other side of the coin from that of the lonely Puritan, hacking his solitary existence out of the world before him, unable to share the awesome burden of individual responsibility, and with no other guide but the cheerless illumination of the light within. Here, by contrast, we have an earnest of that side which admits the appeal of renunciation of personal responsibility; which will gladly accept an imposed discipline.

'They'll have to try', had been Luther's reply in Osborne's play when Cajetan had asked 'How will men find God if they are left to themselves, each man abandoned and known only to himself?' What we see informing Orwell's art is an ac-knowledgement of individual insufficiency or sin; of the almost insupportable weight of the assumed role, and of the whole that has been repudiated. In his last and greatest book, this tension is brought fully into the open and, properly assimi-lated to the moral and aesthetic design, is its true meaning. Less precisely and in a less satisfactorily integrated form it had been anticipated as early as 1996 in *Keep the Aspidistra Flying*; indeed it is basically the same tension that is subsumed in every other book he wrote.

'Faith vanishes but the need for faith remains'. The spiritual continuum is as strongly affirmed in this remark and in Orwell's work generally, as it is in that more political denial of finitude: 'The king is dead, long live the king'. Thus though salvation can now only be had at the cost of a fundamental credal reorientation, salvation is still ardently desired. The growing ambivalence in Orwell's moral vision prepares us for just such a sacrifice; so that we accept as entirely logical indeed as inevitable – the conclusion of *Nineteen Eighty-Four* where the battle of beliefs culminates in unconditional sur-render to the unified command of Priest and Commissar.

It is entirely fitting that, in 'Notes on the Way', Orwell should end by drawing attention with some energy to a notable omission which usually occurs when any reference is made to Marx's well-known comment about religion:

> Marx's famous saying that 'religion is the opium of the people' is habitually wrenched out of its context and given a meaning subtly but appreciably different from the one he gave it. Marx did not say, at any rate in that place, that religion is merely a dope handed out from above; he said that it is something the people create for themselves to supply a need that he recognised to be a real one. 'Religion is the sigh of the soul in a soulless world. Religion is the opium of the people'.[37]

Orwell knew all about the sigh of the soul and about the soul-less world. But instinctively and emotionally he behaves not unlike this own wasp, neither fully admitting the loss of his soul nor entirely giving up all hope that somewhere, somehow, a world-soul is waiting.

The argument of this and other chapters would seem to me to be further vindicated in Malcolm Muggeridge's recent essay in which he quotes a letter from Richard Rees, perhaps Orwell's closest friend:

> I am at the moment engaged in trying to write a longer and better sketch of Eric than the one I wrote shortly after his death in which I try to show that his value consists in his having taken more seriously than most people the funda-mental problem of religion . . . Personally, I think [*Nineteen Eighty-Four*] morbid because he was so ill when he was writing it. But it *does* reveal his true and permanent preoccupat-tion; and that is why I always think of him as a religious or 'pious atheist'.[38]

*   *   *

According to George Woodcock 'the novel in which Orwell had his say about religion' is *A Clergyman's Daughter*.[39] One's immediate reaction to this is to adapt a sentence of E.M. Forster's and say 'Oh dear yes, *A Clergyman's Daughter is* about religion'.

But Professor Woodcock's remark is, in fact, very mislead-ing and it would be compounding a critical felony to fail to take the issue further. Orwell's concern with religion is funda-mental to his creative vision and consequently pervades all his work. *A Clergyman's Daughter* (1935) is not his only statement on the subject; neither is it his most serious, characteristic or creative.

Dorothy Hare, overworked in her role as housekeeper and substitute-curate to her father the Rector of St. Athelstan's is finally submerged beneath the triviality, the meanness and the futility of her apparently endless round of parochial chores. She suffers a complete loss of memory, wanders away from home and in due course ends up in that Orwellian Beulah, the hop-fields of Kent. While there, her memory begins to come back and when she is fully restored she goes home to her father via a lurid *symboliste* experience in Trafalgar Square, and an equally extravagant – though this time Dickensian – set piece in Mrs. Creevy's Academy for Girls. But she returns with her faith demolished, one of the long line of Orwellian prodigals who though coming back, insist upon husks in preference to the fatted calf. The message is loud, clear and stoical; and so is the author:

> She did not reflect, consciously, that the solution to her difficulty lay in accepting the fact that there was no solution; that if one gets on with the job that lies to hand, the ultimate purpose of the job fades into insignificance, that faith and no faith are very much the same provided that one is doing what is customary, useful and acceptable. She could not formulate these thoughts as yet, she could only live them. Much later, perhaps, she would formulate them and draw comfort from them.[40]

The notable austerity of these sentiments is more than a little compromised by the histrionic under-current; and by a self-consciousness which draws attention to the shallowness of the moral philosophy. It calls to mind that even more embarrassing tryout of Stoical Piety in a poem written two years earlier:

> And let us know, as men condemned,
> In peace and thrift of time stand still
> To learn our world while yet we may,
> And shape our souls, however ill;
>
> And we will live, hand, eye and brain,
> Piously, outwardly, ever-aware,
> Till all our hours burn clear and brave
> Like candle flames in windless air;[41]

At any rate, to accept this sententious stiff-upper-lip moralising as Orwell's last word on religion is critically otiose in the particular and indicative of a failure to understand the nature of Orwell's writing in general. The book is palpably a tentative and superficial exploration of 'faith and no faith', as blatantly experimental in its credal position as it is in its conglomerate literary style.

Even if nothing else did, once again the variety of devils would suggest the book's moral uncertainty: at one time he is Baudelairean and at another Faustian – with, in the latter case Mr. Warburton playing the role of a wicked, bottom-pinching Mephistopheles. It is in fact, dramatically clear that Orwell is most at his ease when he gets Dorothy well away from the Rectory:

> Looking back, afterwards, upon her interlude of hop-picking, it was always the afternoons that Dorothy remembered. Those long laborious hours in the strong sunlight, in the sound of forty voices singing, in the smell of hops and wood smoke, had a quality peculiar and unforgettable. As the afternoon wore on you grew almost too tired to stand, and the small green hop lice got into your hair and into your ears and worried you, and your hands, from the sulphurous juice, were as black as a Negro's except where they were bleeding. Yet you were happy, with an unreasonable happiness. The work took hold of you and absorbed you. It was stupid work, mechanical, exhausting, and every day more painful to the hands, and yet you never wearied of it; when the weather was fine and the hops were good you had the feeling that you could go on picking for ever and for ever. It gave you a physical joy, a warm satisfied feeling inside you, to stand there hour after hour, tearing off the heavy clusters and watching the pale green pile grow higher and higher in your bin, every bushel another twopence in your pocket. The sun burned down upon you, baking you brown, and the bitter, never-palling scent, like a wind from oceans of cool beer, flowed into your nostrils and refreshed you.[42]

Given her sheltered background, Dorothy knowledgeably sniffing the winds from oceans of cool beer shows herself unexpectedly seasoned, but at least it supports the impression that Orwell is further inside the experience than he is anywhere else in the book – least of all at the end when Dorothy reflects on her crisis of disillusionment.

Significantly, the final statement is almost literally just that. Dorothy's cogitations on the loss of faith are never assimilated into a work of fiction, with the result that her dilemma never achieves a form likely to make an impact upon the reader's sensibility. So casually rendered is this 'experience' of hers, and so far from being woven into a unifying aesthetic figure which might confer upon it a richer metaphorical life and transform her dilemma into something both substantial and communicable, that the author feels free to break cover virtually at any time:

> For she perceived that in all that happens in church, however absurd and cowardly its supposed purpose may be, there is something – it is hard to define, but something of decency, of spiritual comeliness – that is not easily found in the world outside. It seemed to her that even though you no longer believe, it is better to go to church than not; better to follow in the ancient ways, than to drift in rootless freedom.[43]

Certain thinly disguised authorial statements stand out in a way that recalls the less attractive elements in George Eliot's writing: 'Faith vanishes but the need for faith remains'; 'He was . . . incapable of understanding how a mind naturally pious must recoil from a world discovered to be meaningless'.[44] In their foggy attitudinising such observations strongly suggest a *lack* of commitment in any direction and the basic uncertainty at the core of the author's moral position:

> It was not long before Dorothy found herself in a perpetually low-spirited, jaded state in which, try as she would, nothing seemed able to interest her. And it was in the hateful ennui of this time – the corrupting ennui that lies in wait for every modern soul – that she first came to a full understanding of what it meant to have lost her faith.[45]

We may, of course, against the mass of later evidence, take such po-faced rhetoric as representing Orwell's personal views, as Philip Rieff does when he insists that 'Orwell's answer for Dorothy is his own',* but the meagreness of its aesthetic form would by itself suggest that these views were, at this point, neither stable nor deeply felt.

Interestingly enough, Dorothy is at her most 'real' not in

* See Chapter 3, p

doubt and disillusionment but in her moments of faith. It had been easy for Orwell to laugh off Mrs. Pither's notion of religion:

> Whatever we've suffered, we gets it all back in Heaven, don't we, Miss? Every little bit of suffering, you gets it back a hundredfold and a thousandfold. That *is* true, ain't it, Miss? There's rest for us all in Heaven – rest and peace and no more rheumatism nor digging nor cooking nor laundering nor nothing.[46]

But it is clearly more difficult for him to ridicule Dorothy's mystic pantheism:

> Dorothy caught sight of a wild rose, flowerless of course, growing beyond the hedge, and climbed over the gate with the intention of discovering whether it were not sweetbriar. She knelt down among the tall weeds beneath the hedge. It was very hot down there, close to the ground. The humming of many unseen insects sounded in her ears, and the hot summery fume of the tangled swathes of vegetation flowed up and enveloped her. Near by, tall stalks of fennel were growing, with trailing fronds of foliage like the tails of sea-green horses. Dorothy pulled a frond of the fennel against her face and breathed in the strong sweet scent. Its richness overwhelmed her, almost dizzied her for a moment. She drank it in, filling her lungs with it. Lovely, lovely scent – scent of summer days, scent of childhood joys, scent of spice-drenched islands in the warm foam of oriental seas.
>
> Her heart swelled with sudden joy. It was that mystical joy in the beauty of the earth and the very nature of things that she recognized, perhaps mistakenly, as the love of God. As she knelt there in the heat, the sweet odour and the drowsy hum of insects, it seemed to her that she could momentarily hear the mighty anthem of praise that the earth and all created things send up everlastingly to their maker. All vegetation, leaves, flowers, grass, shining, vibrating, crying out in their joy. Larks also chanting, choirs of larks invisible, dripping music from the sky. All the riches of summer, the warmth of the earth, the song of birds, the fume of cows, the droning of countless bees,

mingling and ascending like the smoke of ever-burning altars.[47]

Her later inclination towards a transcendental idealism is also given a force and an eagerness which leaves a distinct image of her stretching out in appeal towards something which her nature tells her – in defiance of the evidence – is there:

> Since you exist, God must have created you, and since He created you a conscious being, He must be conscious. The greater doesn't come out of the less. He created you, and He will kill you, for His own purpose. But that purpose is inscrutable. It is in the nature of things that you can never discover it, and perhaps even if you did discover it you would be averse to it. Your life and death, it may be, are a single note in the eternal orchestra that plays for His diversion.[48]

Faith vanishes but the need for faith remains, she tells us. What she then goes on to describe is the indestructibility of that urge to spiritual commitment which so strongly infuses Orwell's writing:

> And given only faith, how can anything else matter? How can anything dismay you if only there is some purpose in the world which you can serve, and which, while serving it, you can understand? Your whole life is illumined by that sense of purpose. There is no weariness in your heart, no doubts, no feeling of futility, no Baudelairean ennui waiting for unguarded hours. Every act is significant, every moment sanctified, woven by faith as into a pattern, a fabric of never-ending joy.[49]

This is the language of the soul which ardently desired communion and as such is characteristic of Orwell. It is a language we discover again in *Nineteen Eighty-Four* often couched in very much the same submissive form of self-surrender as, 'He created you, and He will kill you, for His own purpose. But that purpose is inscrutable.' Comparing the intensity of Dorothy's urge towards communion with the portrayal of her disillusionment underlines just how flat and unfelt the latter is. To be told of 'the deadly emptiness that she had discovered at the heart of things' is not enough, yet this mannered and monotonous reportage is really all we are offered. It is certainly not given any greater depth by the invention of the simmering glue-pot, the smell from which was 'the answer to Dorothy's prayer': consistency is maintained there, however, for the device is of precisely the same facile order. Indeed the only image which does have a successful figurative life is the one which shows with unforced irony the futility of Dorothy's existence as she devotes herself to the construction of brown-paper breast-plates, jack-boots and other costumes for yet another pageant. They are as empty of life as she had found herself to be when, after her return from Mr. Warburton, she felt 'in an almost literal sense of the words, washed out'.[50] The shells of life unobtrusively become a correlative of her own spiritual desiccation: her doubt and disillusionment now stifling any capacity she might have had to breathe the spirit into them.

But this is the unique exception. An austere stoicism is all too explicitly the effect being aimed for, but the focus upon it is neither steady nor coherent. As this might imply, the stoicism itself is little more than half-hearted: amongst the compromising elements already referred to there can be detected a strong tendency to fall back upon the rhetorical defences of the Puritan in doubt. Down the ages, *Lord, I believe, Help Thou my unbelief* and *Though He slay me yet will I worship him*, have been the twin texts of the Puritan in trouble with his faith.* More seriously, we have the familiar insistence on the prime virtue of getting on with the job that lies nearest to hand, of committing oneself to 'what is customary, useful and acceptable'. The smell of the glue-pot gratefully inhaled by Dorothy, is the Puritan's incense: it is the odour of sanctity that envelopes the individual who refuses to shirk his duty under any circumstance but soldiers on in his solitary struggle to justify his selection and make himself acceptable in the eye of his remote but demanding Taskmaster. In the last sentence of *A Clergyman's Daughter*, redolent of the Puritan character, we might note especially the word 'pious':

It was beginning to get dark, but, too busy to stop and light

---

* The former text from St. Mark is reputedly the one at which Luther suffered his celebrated fit in the choir. The incident is not well documented.

the lamp, she worked on, pasting strip after strip of paper into place, with absorbed, with pious concentration, in the penetrating smell of the gluepot.

Dorothy – not insignificantly for our appreciation of Orwell – is greatly given to providing scriptural references, and one of these is to St. Luke, Chapter 9, verse 62. What we find there couldn't describe better the spiritual outlook just alluded to:

And Jesus said unto him. No man, having put his hand to the plough, and turning back, is fit for the Kingdom of God.

There is an aptness in this text extending far beyond the char-acterisation of Dorothy Hare and *A Clergyman's Daughter*: it expresses a sentiment quite central to Orwell's moral vision. But in itself it is certainly not that vision, which is, finally, something much larger. For what Orwell confesses is that, however hard individual man tries to keep the text's implicit commandment, and however essential it is for him that he should, he is, in the event, prevented from doing so – and pri-marily by his own nature. He does turn back and thus renders himself unfit for the Kingdom of God. This is at the root of Orwell's crisis of integrity: much as he (and many of his sur-rogates) aspires to be a Daniel, it is the identity of the sinner which has the greater fascination and which he ultimately accepts.

A Clergyman's Daughter is not a good novel but it has been necessary to say this much about it lest George Woodcock's observation should distort our views of the nature and signifi-cance of religion in Orwell's work. His 'say about religion' has, morally and aesthetically, little to do with the glib stoi-cism wished upon Dorothy Hare.

6 Operating in History:
Ethics and Aesthetics

> . . . it is possible to be an atheist, it is possible not to know
> if God exists or why he should, and yet to believe that man
> does not live in a state of nature but in history, and that
> history as we know it now began with Christ, it was
> founded by him on the Gospels.
>
> Nikolay Nikolayevich in Boris Pasternak's *Dr. Zhivago*

> History is the life of mind itself which is not mind except
> so far as it both lives in the historical process and knows
> itself as so living.
>
> R.G. Collingwood

In his essay 'Culture and Democracy' Orwell affirms his belief
in the indissoluble unity of art and life in a single concise sentence: 'Literature as we know it is inseparable from the sanctity of the individual'.[1] His whole position – aesthetic, ethical
and moral – is subsumed in this flat assertion, though there
are many other places where he is equally explicit about the
impossibility of any divorce between art and morality. As he
sees it, both emerge from, and express a part of, some ultimately inarticulable inner self:

> All likes and dislikes, all aesthetic feeling, all notions of
> right and wrong (aesthetic and moral considerations are in
> any case inextricable) spring from feelings which are gener-
> ally admitted to be subtler than words.[2]

A cruder version of the same conviction is to be found in his
remark that 'Few people have the guts to say outright that art
and propaganda are the same thing'.[3]

If Orwell's aesthetic is tied so firmly to the individualist
ethic and the latter is apparently fatally embattled, then literature 'as we know it' is likewise under sentence. The process
of erosion whereby freedom of personal judgement and choice

is lost or squandered is, initially, very much like that described by a character in Pasternak's *Dr. Zhivago*. Lara reveals a consciousness that Orwell himself might have created, and indeed the whole book expresses a vision fundamentally akin to Orwell's.* Reflecting on the unhappy fate that has overtaken herself and her country, Lara concludes:

> It was then that falsehood came into our Russian land. The great misfortune, the root of all the evil to come, was the loss of faith in the value of personal opinions. People imagined that it was out of date to follow their own moral sense, that they must all sing the same tune in chorus, and live by other people's notions, the notions that were being crammed down everybody's throat . . .
> This social evil became an epidemic. It was catching. And it affected everything, nothing was left untouched by it.[4]

Orwell's admonitions and strictures derive their urgency from his having identified the source of nascent infection in precisely the same quarter. Confidence in one's own opinion and one's own moral sense was a *sine qua non* in the affirmation of an individualist ethic against totalitarian absolutism Indeed it is another way of reiterating one's right and duty to prove all things and hold fast to that which is good. As such it justifies man's attempt to find himself in his own expression; from which, as Orwell sees it, has risen the distinctive literature of the last four hundred years:

> . . . in all that we say about literature, and (above all) in all that we say about criticism, we instinctively take the autonomous individual for granted. The whole of modern European literature – I am speaking of the literature of the past four hundred years – is built on the concept of intellectual honesty, or, if you like to put it that way, on Shakespeare's maxim, 'To thine own self be true'.[5]

What we are now entering upon, however – 'the break-up of *laissez-faire* capitalism and of the liberal-Christian culture'[6] – means the decline of the individual's economic freedom and

---

* Certainly much more so than Zamyatin's *We* with which comparisons are normally drawn despite the superficiality of the resemblance.

this in turn, we are told in 'Literature and Totalitarianism', means the restriction of intellectual liberty, since both were the consequence of the fundamental belief in the autonomous individual. The implications for literature are unmistakeable. 'The autonomous individual is going to be stamped out of existence . . . The literature of liberalism is coming to an end and the literature of totalitarianism has not yet appeared and is barely imaginable'.[7] This doom-laden judgement comes from his essay 'Inside the Whale' where he propagates most vigorously and explicitly his vision of a dying Protestant culture. If there should still be some lingering doubts about its being a specifically Protestant culture this essay unsparingly clears them up:

> Literature as we know it is an individual thing, demanding mental honesty and a minimum of censorship. And this is even truer of prose than of verse. It is probably not a coincidence that the best writers of the 'thirties have been poets. The atmosphere of orthodoxy is always damaging to prose, and above all it is completely ruinous to the novel, the most anarchical of all forms of literature. How many Roman Catholics have been good novelists? Even the handful one could name have usually been bad Catholics. The novel is practically a Protestant form of art; it is a product of the free mind, of the autonomous individual.[8]

There will be no 'free mind' and no 'own self' to be true to in the totalitarian world where an identity of *any* sort is entirely conditional upon complete obedience to the prescribed ideological dogma. Orwell's recognition that totalitarianism 'isolates you from the outside world [and] shuts you up in an artificial universe in which you have no standard of comparison'[9] reinforces the importance he attaches to direct contact with an empirically verifiable reality. Literature 'as we know it' is to him very much an expression of this intimacy. It reflects man's right of access to the widest range of consciousness and Orwell quite clearly sees this epitomised in the fullest communication between man's senses and the natural world. As his own writing shows in its occasional Düreresque excess of physical detail his concern for such contact could be obsessive but his failure fully to assimilate the product to his artistic purpose merely reveals how much of the pressure behind that purpose came from precisely this source. So basic was it indeed to his cultural identity and that of his period that literature to be worthy of the name had to reflect it. In his essay 'Lear, Tolstoy and the Fool' Orwell suggests that what Tolstoy so bitterly resents in Shakespeare is the latter's 'tendency to take – not so much a pleasure, as simply an interest in the process of life', Tolstoy's scheme does not allow for this:

> One's interests, one's points of attachment to the physical world and the day-to-day struggle, must be as few and not as many as possible. Literature must consist of parables, stripped of detail and almost independent of language.[10]

It is obvious here that Tolstoy's offence is in overturning not so much Shakespeare's as Orwell's value-system for it is exactly what he is held to repudiate that Orwell affirms – and time and time again in these same terms. A few pages later Shakespeare is praised for embodying very Orwellian virtues: 'he did have curiosity: he loved the surface of the earth and the process of life . . .'[11]. (Interestingly, in an article called 'Will Freedom die with Capitalism?' which appeared in Left News in April 1941, he wrote that man would only find true happiness 'in a society . . . in which men are governed by *love and curiosity* and not by greed and fear'. The italics are mine.)

If Orwell's art and his Protestant, individualist ethic can thus be seen to be inextricable, it still remains to show how this ethic, in all its precariousness, has not only a very particular influence on the form of his work as well as on its content but also inspires the reciprocal functioning of these in a remarkable way. We see this specially exemplified in three books, *Down and Out in Paris and London*, *The Road to Wigan Pier* and *Homage to Catalonia*. In all of these Orwell adopts the role of a rather discursive diarist and the books themselves emerge in a rounded-out diary-form. He is, it seems, recording events and situations, and this, together with the record-form itself, is an assertion of the individual's right and capacity to observe and to make personal judgements. But then we discover that the external world is acting more as a reflector and our attention is refocussed upon that observing self which we took as a datum, or as a *point de départ*. For these books despite their preoccupation with the 'real' world and the recording of it are essentially spiritual autobiographies: explorations of that self which appraise its constitution and the conditions and chances of its survival. Again it is worth drawing attention to Orwell's antecedents here, perhaps best done by quoting from William Haller's *The Rise of Puritanism* where he refers at one point to the diary as 'a Protestant form of art'. In the course of discussing the work of Richard Rogers he enlarges on this:

> The diary, like the autobiography, of which it was the forerunner, was the puritan's confessional. In its pages he could fling upon his God the fear and weakness he found in his heart but would not betray to the world.[12]

A considerable amount of time has already been spent in looking at *Down and Out in Paris and London* and *The Road to Wigan Pier* in this light, but so far nothing has been said about *Homage to Catalonia* which is particularly interesting in the way form and subject are identified. Here Orwell presents himself as something of a war-correspondent, but we soon discover that this is a correspondent who is as interested in his own reaction to events as in the events themselves. Subsequently we come to realise, perhaps with some surprise, just how much emphasis is given to this orientation: for it is not too much to say that to Orwell the reality of a historical event is at least as much in his personal experience and expression of it as in its putative intrinsic 'truth'. How is this reconciled with his championship of, and moral dependence on, 'objective truth'? There is, as it happens, no contradiction; for it neither denies 'fact' nor the concept of objective truth. To the contrary it returns us to a very Protestant position. The objectivity and reality of the external world is accepted and it is the responsibility of the individual to strive to give an account of it and himself in it, true to his only yardstick, the evidence of his own sensations and perceptions. He may not gain general credence for his evaluation but he will have accepted the *concept* of objective truth and in the process fulfilled his responsibility to prove all things, thus displaying the freedom of his personal moral sense.

Turning to *Homage to Catalonia* our first clue to the nature of the book is to be found in the title itself, for what follows is not, in fact, primarily a description of how Catalonia won Orwell's admiration for the spirit that prevailed there during the war. It is expressive of a much more personal debt: a personal gratitude for one more voyage of spiritual self-discovery.

Virtually the last words of *Down and Out in Paris and London* (1933) had expressed Orwell's wish to know people like Mario and Paddy and Bill the Moocher, 'not from casual encounters, but intimately.' *Homage to Catalonia* opens:

> In the Lenin Barracks in Barcelona, the day before I joined the militia, I saw an Italian militiaman standing in front of the officers' table.

The soldier 'a tough-looking youth of twenty-five or six, with reddish-yellow hair and powerful shoulders' makes an immediate impression on Orwell:

> Something in his face deeply moved me. It was the face of a man who would commit murder and throw away his life for a friend . . . There were both candour and ferocity in it; also the pathetic reverence that illiterate people have for their supposed superiors.

A brief exchange follows between them and as he leaves, the Italian crosses the room and grips Orwell's hand 'very hard':

> It was as though his spirit and mine had momentarily succeeded in bridging the gulf of language and tradition and meeting in utter intimacy.[13]

Not only can this be seen as a consummation of the desire voiced at the end of the earlier book, it also gives some indication of what he really sought there. It was Catalonia in wartime which provided for him the ideal community in which he could find, and come to terms with, himself: the only time that he did so despite his strenuous efforts among the down-and-out. Of his three or four months in the line he wrote:

> They formed a kind of interregnum in my life quite different from anything that had gone before and perhaps from anything that is to come, and they taught me things that I could never have learned in any other way.[14]

Now he was one of a community in which he could be accepted at once and merge with the rest. There was no class-
barrier here to be resurrected in a give-away Etonian vowel.
The militiaman's action had been a witness of that and
Orwell, responding to his initiative with a transcendent,
almost sensual ardour, experiences an instantaneous but profound communion. Division, or as we can perhaps now more
clearly see, self-division is overcome; the devil being exorcised
in his familiar form of class-distinction:

> The ordinary class division of society had disappeared to an
> extent that is almost unthinkable in the money-tainted air of
> England; there was no one there except the peasants and
> ourselves, and no one owned anyone else as his master. Of
> course such a state of affairs could not last. It was simply a
> temporary and local phase in an enormous game that is
> being played over the whole surface of the earth.[15]

'Of course it could not last, for it was, for Orwell, more a hint
of the promised land than Canaan itself. He had been vouchsafed a glimpse in reality of the 'Golden Country' he refers to
in *Nineteen Eighty-Four* and, so fortified, could commit himself
gratefully to the community which had allowed him his revelation:

> However much one cursed at the time, one realised after-
> wards that one had been in contact with something
> strange and valuable. One had been in a community
> where hope was more normal than apathy or cynicism,
> where the word 'comrade' stood for comradeship and not,
> as in most countries, for humbug. One had breathed the
> air of equality . . . For the Spanish militias, while they
> lasted, were a sort of microcosm of a classless society. In
> that community where no one was on the make, where
> there was a shortage of everything but no privilege and no
> boot-licking, one got, perhaps a crude forecast of what the
> opening stages of Socialism might be like.[16]

But it could not last: the clouds had simply parted momen-
tarily to let him see that his dreams *could* be fulfilled. Even
the militiaman's gesture, after the instinctive response, was

treasured for its ideal truth rather than as the harbinger of a brave new world. Immediately after their meeting 'in utter intimacy', Orwell adds:

> But I also knew that to retain my first impression of him I must not see him again.[17]

And the militiaman, with his 'crystal spirit' intact, joins the paper weight of *Nineteen Eighty-Four* and the secret pool with its enormous carp in *Coming Up for Air*, as an image of that private, interior life now under sentence. Two years after 'when the war was visibly lost', Orwell wrote some verses in the militiaman's memory which included the lines:

> The Italian soldier shook my hand
> Beside the guard-room table;
> The strong hand and the subtle hand
> Whose palms are only able
>
> To meet within the sound of guns,
> But oh! what peace I knew then
> In gazing on his battered face
> Purer than any woman's!
>
> * * *
>
> Your name and your deeds were forgotten
> Before your bones were dry,
> And the lie that slew you is buried
> Under a deeper lie;
>
> But the thing that I saw in your face
> No power can disinherit:
> No bomb that ever burst
> Shatters the crystal spirit.[18]

Orwell's search for the face that showed sympathy and understanding was extraordinarily consistent and for a moment he found it in this man in whose soul his own discovered an identity. The moment of truth passes but it has done its work and colours even his dreary experience at the front:

> This period which then seemed so futile and eventless is now of great importance to me. It is so different from the

rest of my life that already it has taken on the magic quality which, as a rule, belongs only to memories that are years old.[19]

That such a moment could only be found 'within the sound of guns' is no less inevitable than its evanescence – indeed it is entirely symptomatic of the transience and vulnerability which it was bound to have in Orwell's eyes. What is both particularly moving and dramatically apt in the incident is that its affirmation is made with the forces of destruction poised for the kill: its principals in uniform but woefully ill-equipped for the struggle. Outside their ranks a world conspires to misrepresent and ultimately destroy. All that in Orwell's view constitutes humanity and decency has been forced right to the brink, fighting a rear-guard action with its back to the abyss: it is inspiring but, like the position of the zealots at Masada, in the highest degree critical.

What Orwell does so well in *Homage to Catalonia* is to give us a three-dimensional representation of the crisis in what purports to be a two-dimensional form. His concern with the documentary is far from being simply that of the journalist or war-correspondent, whose objective is primarily to give an authentic picture of what is going on or has gone on in the theatre of action. If we take it as such it is difficult to avoid the conclusions of the reviewer in *The Listener* who described the book as 'a muddle-headed and inaccurate political treatise' where there is

> scarcely a page of political disquisition in which [Orwell] does not admit that he may be mistaken or that he is presenting hearsay from sources which he believes – but does not know – to be reliable.[20]

What he is really concerned with is being true to his own unmediated sensations and perceptions and in being so to assert his fundamental principle that the individual's capacity to exercise this freedom is a condition and a guarantee of his individuality. One man's ability and will to do so in the context of the Civil War where the main contenders made such strenuous efforts to falsify the record was worth far more than the most carefully balanced and researched assessment. His conclusions may indeed have been 'wrong' or inaccurate but his free statement of his own observation and judgement, the products of direct confrontation, were a refusal to be an accomplice in the falsification, and a guarantee that truth *could* be pursued and even attained – and that the individual could survive. In 'The Prevention of Literature' he is quite explicit about it:

> Although other aspects of the question are usually in the foreground the controversy over freedom of speech and of the press is at the bottom a controversy over the desirability, or otherwise, of telling lies. What is really at issue is the right to report contemporary events truthfully, or as truthfully as is consistent with the ignorance, bias and self-deception from which every observer necessarily suffers.[21]

Obviously he was fully aware that his own reporting of the war was both inadequate and biased and he is continually warning us of the fact: 'I warn everyone against my bias, and I warn everyone against my mistakes. Still, I have done my best to be honest'.[22] He, at least, is *trying* to be truthful (and from this cardinal virtue of being true to his own perceptions comes his dogged, and at times, lugubrious honesty), whereas, with Fascist propaganda about the war in mind, in all around him 'the very concept of objective truth is fading out of the world'.[23] So that in going to considerable lengths to expound the complexity of the parties involved, he is simultaneously offering an example of what it is he is affirming: the fundamental importance to the individual of the concept of objective truth. *Homage to Catalonia* is very much of a piece and Orwell was quite right to reject the advice of those who would have had him cut out the material which sought to define the obscure political anatomy of the revolution.

Very significantly, he places the incident with the militiaman at the beginning of the story: this was the moment of vision, of communion and rededication before the battle, bringing the peace that passes understanding. But it really is more than this, for the terms used to describe this meeting 'in utter intimacy' sanctify the experience to a degree that makes the spirit affirmed in man predicate Spirit. It asserts a dimension inherent in human nature which, in its mystery and immortality, comes to appear as soul *incognito*. What then follows is, in form and content, a definition of what is in his view the essential prerequisite for the survival of that spirit or soul. In a history which so vividly deals with the present we have, first, a glimpse of that long-enduring ideal, the dignity and worth of the individual self with its all-important spiritual core still before us as a powerful inspiration, still the hope, albeit beleaguered, of the future. Then comes a demonstration of those powers and faculties without whose free operation Orwell could not see self or soul surviving. But the individual's capacity to unravel and evaluate the present is, we must notice, an explicit recognition of the profound significance to him of the past. The point is made with great cogency in 'Looking Back on the Spanish War' (written in 1942):

> I know it is the fashion to say that most of recorded history is lies anyway. I am willing to believe that history is for the most part inaccurate and biased, but what is peculiar to our own age is the abandonment of the idea that history *could* be truthfully written. In the past people deliberately lied, or they unconsciously coloured what they wrote, or they struggled after the truth, well knowing that they must make many mistakes; but in each case they believed that 'the facts' existed and were more or less discoverable. And in practice there was always a considerable body of fact which would have been agreed to by almost everyone . . . It is just this common basis of agreement, with its implication that human beings are all one species of animal, that totalitarianism destroys. Nazi theory indeed specifically denies that such a thing as 'the truth' exists. There is, for instance, no such thing as 'science'. There is only 'German Science', 'Jewish Science', etc. The implied objective of this line of thought is a nightmare world in which the Leader, or some ruling clique, controls not only the future but *the past*. If the Leader says of such and such an event, 'It never happened' – well, it never happened. If he says that two and two are five – well, two and two are five.[24]

If the individual is the measure and the measurer of all things then he needs history in which to establish himself. The nightmare world Orwell envisages here is so because in it the individual will be prevented from exercising his personal judgement on his own observation: denied access to that\empirical method upon which his moral and spiritual survival depends no less than it does upon contact with nature in the shape of the material world.

Thus in writing so meticulously about the present in *Homage to Catalonia*, Orwell firmly states his belief in the importance and sanctity of the past. History and historiography (to include the contemporary account) are the signature of the individual, and as such, naturally, the object of the totalitarians' attack. He describes their attitude succinctly in 'The Prevention of Literature':

> From the totalitarian point of view history is something to be created rather than learned. A totalitarian state is in effect a theocracy, and its ruling caste, in order to keep its position, has to be thought of as infallible. But since, in practice, no one is infallible, it is frequently necessary to rearrange past events in order to show that this or that mistake was not made, or that this or that imaginary triumph actually happened . . . Totalitarianism demands, in fact the continuous alteration of the past, and in the long run probably demands a disbelief in the very existence of objective truth.[25]

And once again Orwell is being entirely true to his tradition Here is Friedenthal on Luther and the historians:

> The historians, who now make their appearance alongside the jurists, supported the new faith almost to a man. They were constantly producing new material on the conflicts between the emperors and the popes, the disputes of the Councils, the popes and anti-popes, the fearful charges of corruption against the clergy in every century. Hitherto history had meant Church history or history written by priests. Now laymen began to write history . . .[26]

Friedenthal instances Aventin and Sebastian Franck, 'very independent in his viewpoint and critique of human activity', who sought to extract from the multiplicity of events what he

called their 'inner core and binding thongs'. But the significance of their irruption is perhaps as well illustrated in the
latter-day hostility of Cardinal Manning:

> It was the charge of the Reformers that the Catholic doc-
> trines were not primitive, and their pretension was to revert
> to antiquity. But the appeal to antiquity is both a treason
> and a heresy. It is a treason because it rejects the Divine
> voice of the Church at this hour, and a heresy because it
> denies that voice to be Divine. How can we know what anti-
> quity was except through the Church?[27]

The importance, the vulnerability and the preservation of
the spiritual integrity reattested in the epiphany whose
description starts the book is what *Homage to Catalonia* is
about: and in its art as well as its *exempla* it describes the
necessary conditions of its survival.

The constituent which has most to do with expanding the
two- to the three-dimensional is, of course, the dramatically active and involved sensibility of Orwell, so fully and roundly
created that we must again refer to its owner as 'Orwell'. This,
together with the book's driving and controlling faith is the
means by which we have communicated to us the felt reality of
spiritual self-realisation and integrity; and see bathed in
reflected light the cold alternative world of loneliness, uncertainty and alienation. It is the dramatically active self of
'Orwell' which succeeds in fusing the observed data, the act of
observation, the documenting of it, and the concept of the
autonomous individual into a full and subtle expression of one
man's moral vision. Only in the dimension of the imaginary,
says Nicola Chiaromonte, do we learn something real about
individual experience; it is a dimension which informs the
whole of *Homage to Catalonia* in its careful structuring and in
the moral enlargement implicit in 'Orwell's' sensibility.

The conclusion to *Homage to Catalonia* is not pessimistic.
('Curiously enough the whole episode has left me with not less
but more belief in the decency of human beings'.) Indeed, the
whole book is spiritually more reminiscent of the road to
Damascus than the tortuous road to Wigan Pier, though what
it records is not so much a conversion as Orwell's gratitude (or
homage?) for having been vouchsafed a Sign which revivifies

and nourishes an embattled faith and offers him a communion that does not demand self-destruction as a pre-condition.

Nevertheless, if the conclusion is not pessimistic it is deeply anxious. The book ends with 'Orwell' translated back to England – and back, it would seem in time. Here, traditional patterns are complacently accepted by a country quite unaware of their true significance and thus all the more vulnerable to those emerging powers whose precise aim it is to dislodge the individual from his anchorage in the past and from his full consciousness of the world about him. And once again Orwell succeeds in giving greater depth and resonance to the observation by showing that this is also 'Orwell's' own past – the past from which, so to speak, he rode out to the wars, there to be awakened to its true importance and its peril. The ending serves to underline the book's remarkable artistic unity which derives in such measure from the dramatically active 'self' so surely and effectively promoting the moral expansion of the war-correspondent's art:

> The industrial towns were far away, a smudge of smoke and misery hidden by the curve of the earth's surface. Down here it was still the England I had known in my childhood: the railway-cuttings smothered in wild flowers, the deep meadows where the great shining horses browse and meditate, the slow-moving streams bordered by willows, the green bosoms of the elms, the larkspurs in the cottage gardens; and then the huge peaceful wilderness of outer London, the barges on the miry river, the familiar streets, the posters telling of cricket matches and Royal weddings, the men in bowler hats, the pigeons in Trafalgar Square, the red buses, the blue policemen – all sleeping the deep, deep sleep of England, from which I sometimes fear that we shall never awake till we are jerked out of it by the roar of bombs.

*   *   *

The significance of *Homage to Catalonia's* argument and form can now be more clearly discerned. It is a book which opens with an incandescent flash of human love putting beyond question the dignity, the worth, and the *immortality* of mankind. Nikolay Nikolayevich in the rest of the speech from which the

quotation at the head of this chapter is taken goes on to talk
about history and the individual:

> Now what is history? Its beginning is that of the centuries of
> systematic work devoted to the solution of the enigma of
> death, so that death itself may eventually be overcome. This
> is why people write symphonies, and why they discover
> mathematical infinity and electromagnetic waves. Now,
> you can't advance in this direction without a certain
> upsurge of spirit. You can't make such discoveries without
> spiritual equipment, and for this, everything necessary has
> been given us in the Gospels. What is it? Firstly, the love of
> one's neighbour . . . secondly, the two concepts which are
> the make-up of modern man – without them he is inconcei-
> vable – the ideas of free personality and of life regarded as
> sacrifice.[28]

A little later in *Dr. Zhivago* the same character is once more
trying to explain his belief to an unsympathetic listener who,
symptomatically, fails to understand a word of what he is
saying:

> – what has for centuries raised man above the beast is not
> the cudgel but an inward music: the irresistible power of
> unarmed truth, the attraction of its example. It has always
> been assumed that the most important things in the
> Gospels are the ethical teaching and commandments. But
> for me the most important thing is the fact that Christ
> speaks in parables taken from daily life, that he explains the
> truth in terms of everyday reality. *The idea which underlies this
> is that communion between mortals is immortal, and that the whole of
> life is symbolic because the whole of it has meaning.*[29]

The last sentence (which I have italicised) brilliantly sums up
the 'individualist' Orwell when his heart was lightest and his
championship at its most ardent and unequivocal. It articu-
lates the connection which in part motivated his attempts to
meet people 'intimately' amongst the unemployed in Wigan,
the destitute and exploited in London and Paris, as well as in
the ranks of the revolutionaries in Spain. But only in the case
of the last-mentioned did he achieve success when he had his
sudden revelation of the immortality of communion between

mortals in his encounter with the militiaman; and when he discovered dramatic reassurance that life was indeed greater than the sum of its material parts. The brevity of his communion was inevitable for, as we have seen, the conviction behind it was in competition with another, which was that such communion is not enough. The only meaningful communion ultimately (although foreshadowed from the beginning) is one in which the individual will be assimilated completely to a larger identity, and his individuality obliterated.

In the Catalonian community at war 'Orwell' certainly, and Orwell to all appearances, discover communion and the immortality of communion in love for one's fellows and in self sacrifice: all based on a firm belief in the ideal value of the individual human being. But *Homage to Catalonia* makes it abundantly clear that such a basis (and such meaning and communion) is only possible if there is free access for the individual to nature – as we have seen in an earlier chapter – and to history.

What, so to speak, released man into the stream of history (from which, incidentally, Winston Smith foresees it is his doom to be removed, and O'Brien promises him no less) was the liberal-Christian era; by which Orwell meant the Protestant reformation as he interpreted it. More cautiously, Pasternak has his character trace the development to the foundation of Christianity; but the point these two authors are making is the same. 'Christianity' for Pasternak, 'Protestantism' for Orwell, provided an absolute guarantee of man's innate individual worth. With Christ comes an *enduring* place for newly-dignified man *in time*:

'Rome was a flea market of borrowed gods and conquered peoples, a bargain basement on two tiers – earth and heaven – slaves on one, gods on the other . . .'
'And then, into this tasteless heap of gold and marble, He came, light-footed and clothed in light, with his marked humanity, his deliberate Galilean provincialism, and from that moment there was neither gods nor peoples, there was only man – man the carpenter, man the ploughman, man the shepherd with his flock of sheep at sunset, man whose name does not sound in the least proud but who is sung in

lullabies abd portrayed in picture galleries the world over.[30]

Men may die but man does not: he is possessed of a spirit, authenticated by Christ, that conveys itself from generation to generation endowing the present with meaning and the future with hope; seeing to its own celebration by liberating man's creative faculty to spread its gospel. Symphonies will be written that testify to the resources of this spirit and men will search for and discover mathematical infinity. Orwell characteristically sees man coming fully into his spiritual inheritance only after the Reformation has freed him from the absolutist authority of the Roman Catholic church, but his instinctive way of looking at man is very much the one expressed – with the t's crossed and the i's dotted – in Nikolayevitch's reflections:

> It was not until after the coming of Christ that time and man could breathe freely. It was not until after Him that men began to live in their posterity and ceased to die in ditches like dogs – instead, they died, at home in history, at the height of the work they devoted to the conquest of death, being themselves dedicated to this aim . . .[31]

In this view history is the mystery of personality and the writing of history is not, finally, the nailing down of objective fact but the active proof of an individual sensibility. Facts, says Zhivago, don't exist 'until man puts into them something of his own, some measure of his own wilful, human genius . . .' And Misha Gordon in the course of his reply takes up the point:

> 'What the Gospels tell us is that in this new way of life and of communion, which is born of the heart and which is called the Kingdom of God there are no nations, but only persons.'
>
> 'Now you said that facts don't mean anything by themselves – not until a meaning is put into them. Well – the meaning you have to put into the facts to make them relevant to human beings is just that: it's Christianity, it's the mystery of personality . . .'

Orwell's 'factual' record of the Spanish Civil War would seem

to me to be just this: an expression of the mystery of personality. And, as such, just what he meant it to be.

To Orwell it is paramount that the individual should recognise that he – all that is immortal in him – lives within history.
Only in history has he a future as an independent being of
intrinsic worth. But here is the rub: awareness of this fact in
the present day may well show him how tenuous is his place
there, or even that he is doomed to be dislodged. For the guarantor of that intrinsic value is now discredited, and with him
goes the belief on which, as Orwell saw it, Western civilisation
rested: the belief in the immortality of the soul.

Having recognised the importance to Orwell of living within
history, we will be less likely to underestimate the reference to
time which prefaces every one of his major books:

The rue du Coq d'Or, Paris, seven in the morning.
                                    (*Down and Out in Paris and London*)

U Po. Kyin, Sub-divisional Magistrate of Kyauktada in
Upper Burma, was sitting in his veranda. It was only half
past eight, but the month was April . . .
                                    (*Burmese Days*)

As the alarm clock on the chest of drawers exploded like a
horrid little bomb of metal . . .
                                    (*A Clergyman's Daughter*)

The clock struck half past two.
                                    (*Keep the Aspidistra Flying*)

The first sound in the morning was the clumping of the
mill-girls clogs down the cobbled street.
                                    (*The Road to Wigan Pier*)

In the Lenin Barracks in Barcelona, the day before I joined
the militia . . .
                                    (*Homage to Catalonia*)

Mr. Jones, of the Manor Farm, had locked the hen-houses
for the night . . .
                                    (*Animal Farm*)

It was a bright cold day in April and the clocks were striking thirteen.

Keep the Aspidistra Flying not only opens with the familiar reference but, as befits its subject, reflects throughout an almost
Faustian preoccupation with time:

> Down in Mrs. Wisbeach's lair the clock struck half past ten.
> You could always hear it striking at night. Ping-ping, ping-
> ping – a note of doom! The ticking of the alarm clock on the
> mantlepiece became audible to Gordon again, bringing
> with it the consciousness of the sinister passage of
> time . . . Another evening wasted. Hours, days, years slip-
> ping by.
> . . . . . .
> The clock downstairs struck eleven.
> . . . . . .
> The clock struck twelve.[33]

The day-of-doom aspect of this concern with time is, of course,
itself characteristic of Orwell and his heritage. We are recalled
to the task – a little guiltily, too, perhaps – with a reawakened
conscience, and a greater sense of urgency in our sharpened
appreciation that the shining hour that waits improvement
will *not* wait. Such allusions may be thought superficial: the
Puritan's answer to *mañana*. Nevertheless they are
symptomatic, showing that Orwell locates his people strictly
and precisely in time.

In a more important sense man *and* artist, for Orwell, are
unequivocally in time. it is the only place for him if he would
save his individual being; but as such he is a symptom of his
cultural epoch and vulnerable along with it. At his best, writing consciously from within time. Orwell makes it clear that
in these terms there can be no distinction between the creative
writer and experiencing man.

Therefore he, the author, remains the subject, or at any rate
the experiencing observer in the thick of events, to whom
things happen just as they do to everyone else. So he is at
pains to keep before us a sense of the writer's self overtly active
and experiencing. But, of course, there is an element of
double-bluff, for he deepens the impact of the experience
before us by unobtrusively allowing that self to develop a rich

and expanding sensibility; so conferring upon it in its context many of the rhetorical advantages of the fictive persona. To all appearances this is the author but there is a power and a subtlety about his 'personal account' which derives in considerable measure from persona-creation. This 'self' becomes a living organism with its own laws and probabilities, so suggesting a created sensibility from which the author is distanced. It is a technique which is peculiarly Orwell's and we see it at work in *Down and Out in Paris and London*, *The Road to Wigan Pier*, and *Homage to Catalonia*.

With the wholly fictional persona he is much more uncomfortable for it enjoins much too strict and complete a separation to allow him to practise his particular illusion. He is clearly ill-at-ease when he is required to pretend that the author and the *dramatis personae* are wholly distinct. Significantly the best novels are *Coming Up for Air* where the autobiographical 'I' at least gives more of the appearance of identity between writer and actively experiencing character – the 'I', George Bowling, also being almost wholly concerned with his reactions to his experience – and *Nineteen Eighty-Four*. This last is a book with only one character, who seems to me precisely to express Orwell's own predicament. Indeed, it could be argued from his literary insubstantiality that he does so too precisely; that he stays with us as a *voice* rather than a character.

An obvious omission from the list is *Animal Farm* which is entirely successful, even though in the genre of satirical allegory a consistent position for the author outside the action is obligatory. In actual fact, however, the author is anything but remote from the theatre he describes for, being a parable, there is a one-for-one equation between the action and the author's moral vision. The result is an enhancement of the art of the book, for while this vision directs the central irony with rigorous conciseness and economy, at the same time it allows to accrue round it sufficient detail and allusion to move the reader to the realisation that the moral conflict embodied in the fable affects him deeply and intimately.

As the vehicle for his satire the pastoral fable is peculiarly suited to Orwell, since it both disciplines his polemical urge, making it more of a creative instrument, and permits him to infuse into it the warmth of his deep attachment to the flora and fauna of the countryside. Indeed *Animal Farm* as well as being a political satire is a small-scale tragedy of corrupted pastoral. When the animals free themselves from the tyranny of Jones what they attempt to reassert is the fundamental harmony, unity and dignity of the natural world which had been destroyed by un-natural (or de-natured) man. The opening description of the assembly of animals is full of the animals' concern for each other. The two horses, Boxer and Clover, enter together 'walking very slowly and setting down their vast hairy hoofs with great care lest there should be some small animal concealed in the straw.' Shortly after, a brood of duck-lings 'which had lost their mother' file into the barn 'cheeping feebly and wandering from side to side to find some place where they would not be trodden on':

> Clover made a sort of wall round them with her great foreleg, and the ducklings nestled down inside it, and promptly fell asleep.[34]

Lastly the cat comes in and, looking for the warmest place, squeezes herself in between Boxer and Clover: 'there she purred contentedly throughout Major's speech without listen-ing to a word of what he was saying'.

The most complete and attractive picture of this solidarity is the carefully composed scene (reminiscent of an American 'primitive' in its harmony, freshness and innocence) when the animals waken on the first day of their new freedom:

> . . . they awoke at dawn as usual, and suddenly remember-ing the glorious thing that had happened, they all raced out into the pasture together. A little way down the pasture there was a knoll that commanded a view of most of the farm. The animals rushed to the top of it and gazed round them in the clear morning light. Yes, it was theirs – every-thing that they could see was theirs! In the ecstasy of that thought they gambolled round and round, they hurled themselves into the air in great leaps of excitement. They rolled in the dew, they cropped mouthfuls of the sweet summer grass, they kicked up clods of the black earth and snuffed its rich scent. Then they made a tour of inspection

of the whole farm and surveyed with speechless admiration the ploughland, the hayfield, the orchard, the pool, the spinney. It was as though they had never seen these things before, and even now they could hardly believe that it was all their own.[35]

It is on this knoll that the animals' greatest practical achievement is to be erected, but by the time the windmill finally gets built the triumph is altogether hollow, for the harmony and unity of the earlier moment exists no longer. After Napoleon's mass-executions, in defiance of one of the original commandments that 'No animal shall kill any other animal' it is to the knoll that the survivors retreat – in a state of mind starkly contrasted with their earlier exhilaration:

> They had made their way on to the little knoll where the half-finished windmill stood, and with one accord they all lay down as though huddling together for warmth. . . .
> The knoll where they were lying gave them a wide prospect across the countryside. Most of Animal Farm was within their view – the long pasture stretching down to the main road, the hayfield, the spinney, the drinking pool, the ploughed fields where the young wheat was thick and green, and the red roofs of the farm buildings with the smoke curling from the chimneys. It was a clear spring evening. The grass and the bursting hedges were gilded by the level rays of the sun . . . As Clover looked down the hillside her eyes filled with tears.

Explicitly their former brotherhood is invoked:

> If [Clover] herself had had any picture of the future, it had been of a society of animals set free from hunger and the whip, all equal, each working according to this capacity, the strong protecting the weak, as she had protected the last brood of ducklings with her foreleg on the night of Major's speech.[36]

Through the exploitation of the pastoral image, *Animal Farm* describes with force and poignancy the deep desire for unity and the removal of all barriers that has been noted in other books. As on those other occasions it is a desire doomed to disappointment, and the book ends with the pigs becoming totally indistinguishable from man, their former tyrant, before the appalled eyes of the animals peering in through the farm-house window.

Not only are the animals thus betrayed by their own kind; the dénouement suggests – striking a chord by now familiar to us – that such betrayal is an inescapable part of 'their' moral condition. 'It must be due to some fault in ourselves',[37] says Boxer in the traumatic aftermath of the executions, no more able than the other animals to reconcile what he has just witnessed with the idealism that had inspired their rebellion. Inherent in this pastoral world there is, it would appear, a fatal flaw precluding unity and harmony: a flaw ultimately to be located in the very nature of the creatures which inhabit it. The promise in Major's song of 'the golden future time' will never – *can* never – be fulfilled and by the end of the 'fairy story', as *Animal Farm* is sub-titled, it is as much a nostalgic dream as 'the Golden Country' is in *Nineteen Eighty-Four*.

With the brief – and illusory – escape into the countryside of Winston Smith and Julia, the pastoral ideal is finally eclipsed in *Nineteen Eighty-Four*, where 'the last man in Europe' (the original title) quite explicitly surrenders his 'humanistic' faith. It was a faith which, amongst other things, had allowed a language and a literature to flourish whose corruption now, as it is centrally described in the book, signifies the extinction of their moral and ethical foundations. It is the actualisation of the development forecast in those references quoted at the beginning of this chapter to the imminent destruction of literature 'as we know it': a literature, we remember, which emblemised a particular style of integrity, a particular self-system.

Thus there is extreme irony in the last surviving example of that literature – 'the book' passed on by O'Brien – being used successfully to tempt Winston beyond redemption. To accept and read 'the book', so careful an historical account of the past, is a last communion for the individual with his heretical faith. Quite simply, it is to die: as he finishes reading in it, Winston concludes that though he would not survive to see hope for a better future fulfilled, yet it was possible to share in it vicariously if one 'kept alive the mind . . . and passed on the secret doctrine that two plus two make four'. His next remark,

'We are the dead' is therefore not despairing. But the mocking echo from the concealed telescreen at precisely this moment of re-affirmation of the humanistic, rationalistic doctrine, shatters completely all hope as it concurs with a quite different emphasis, 'You are the dead'.[38]

Before considering *Nineteen Eighty-Four*, however, another novel which anticipates it in several important respects merits attention. *Coming Up for Air* followed *Homage to Catalonia* a year later in 1939, and in important ways resembles it closely, for it is a more traditional fictionalising of the same basic credal concern. Here it is George Bowling who plays the role of the embattled individualist, anxiously examining the question of his faith's survival. Reiterating the fundamental importance to individual integrity of direct contact with the external world, and of the truthful recording of sensations, he also lays great stress on the value of the past, and in a way which again shows the connection with the previous book. To Bowling the past is the lockfast accumulation of the records of his and other individuals' contemporary experience: it is a sort of bank of sensations and perceptions into which the individual puts his moral capital for the benefit of his heirs – though he himself draws interest in the shape of the necessary reassurance of individual integrity.

Once again in *Coming Up for Air* Orwell has his chief character show himself acutely conscious of living in time; indeed, the book opens with a double reference to the fact entirely integral to the book's substance:

> The idea really came to me the day I got my new false teeth.
> I remember the morning well. At about a quarter to eight I'd nipped out of bed and got into the bathroom just in time to shut the kids out.

George Bowling's sharp awareness of the moment enables him to see himself with a certain detachment trapped in the narrow end of a dwindling perspective. Behind him, there is the spaciousness of his childhood and youth; before him, the suffocating constriction of life with the mean and nagging Hilda, and the certainty of international war. Blended with his personal, Bloom-like odyssey there is a deeper concern with past, present and future, and it is this which, on the whole, neutralises the sentimental nostalgia, and makes the book an obvious and not unworthy successor to *Homage to Catalonia*.

The close attention which Bowling bestows upon his own body is characteristic of his deep, rather indulgent but far from trivial interest in himself as an individual and in his own responses. Artistically, this interest is well-modulated, allowing us on occasion to move close in to the physicality of this particular man and on others to keep far enough away to see him as part of a larger temporal process. Then George Bowling becomes a kind of prism through which time appears in highly corporeal fragments:

> I soaped my arms (I've got those kind of pudgy arms that are freckled up to the elbow) and then took the back-brush and soaped my shoulder-blades, which in the ordinary way I can't reach. It's a nuisance, but there are several parts of my body that I can't reach nowadays. The truth is that I'm inclined to be a little bit on the fat side.[39]

He sets out for town with a soapy patch on the back of his neck:

> That sticky feeling round my neck had put me into a demoralized kind of mood. It's curious how it gets you down to have a sticky neck. It seems to take all the bounce out of you, like when you suddenly discover in a public place that the sole of one of your shoes is coming off. I had no illusions about myself that morning. It was almost as if I could stand at a distance and watch myself coming down the road, with my fat, red face and my false teeth and my vulgar clothes.[40]

It is part of the book's success as a fictional autobiography that Bowling conveys an impression of honesty in his own observations together with a very considerable degree of self-awareness.

In fact, in *Coming Up for Air* there is a well-integrated dramatisation of a by now very familiar structure, though here the past plays a larger role than it did elsewhere with the exception of *Homage to Catalonia*. In his quiet appraisal of himself at forty-five, Bowling places himself very firmly in the natural world and defines himself by the precision of his observation. His senses are immensely alive and his recapitulation of the early product of this faculty is convincing simply because it leaves the impression of a human being fully conscious of the world around him and savouring every morsel of experience. His reprise has an intensity that gains from his disparagement of facile sentiment – 'that poetry of childhood stuff' – being placed side by side with an idyllic rendering of the ecstatic pleasure he got as a boy from fishing:

> The truth is that kids aren't in any way poetic, they're merely savage little animals, except that no animal is a quarter as selfish. A boy isn't interested in meadows, groves and so forth. He never looks at a landscape, doesn't give a damn for flowers . . . Killing things – that's about as near to poetry as a boy gets. And yet all the while there's that peculiar intensity, the power of longing for things as you can't long when you're grown up, and the feeling that time stretches out and out in front of you . . . [41]

The description of his first fishing-trip is extraordinarily good and all the more so since in this hand-to-hand encounter with nature the boy is initiated into something more than the art of fishing; the whole experience is suffused with his own growing-up:

> . . . the next moment there wasn't any doubt about it. The float dived straight down, I could still see it under the water, kind of dim red, and I felt the rod tighten in my hand. Christ, that feeling! The line jerking and straining and a fish on the other end of it! The others saw my rod bending and the next moment they'd all flung their rods down and rushed round to me. I gave a terrific haul and the fish – a great huge silvery fish – came flying up through the air. The same moment all of us gave a yell of agony. The fish had slipped off the hook and fallen into the wild peppermint under the bank. But he'd fallen into shallow water where he couldn't turn over, and for perhaps a second he lay there on his side helpless. Joe flung himself into the water, splashing us all over, and grabbed him in both hands. 'I got 'im!' he yelled. The next moment he'd flung

the fish on to the grass and we were all kneeling round it. How we gloated! The poor dying brute flapped up and down and his scales glistened all the colours of the rainbow. It was a huge carp, seven inches long at least, and must have weighed a quarter of a pound. How we shouted to see him! But the next moment it was as though a shadow had fallen across us. We looked up, and there was old Brewer standing over us, with his tall billy-cock hat – one of those hats they used to wear that were a cross between a top-hat and a bowler – and his cowhide gaiters and a thick hazel in his hand.

We suddenly cowered like partridges when there's a hawk overhead. He looked from one to other of us. He had a wicked old mouth with no teeth in it, and since he'd shaved his beard off his chin looked like a nut-cracker.[42]

The passage is well worth quoting in full for in its communication of the excitement, the sense of suddenly realised physical prowess as well as fledgling vulnerability, it is an excellent portrayal of the boy's growth in nature. Orwell's skill in manipulating Bowling's perspective is well illustrated in the placing of the words man, kid, boy, in the conclusion to the description, where Bowling, characteristically insists on doing the fullest justice to his feeling:

I had a wonderful feeling inside me, a feeling you can't know about unless you've had it – but if you're a man you'll have had it some time. I knew that I wasn't a kid any longer, I was a boy at last.[43]

But the shadow that falls over them is more sinister than merely that of old Brewer (before whom they 'cowered like partridges when there's a hawk overhead'), and it links Bowling's threatened youth with a threatened civilisation. Later he is standing by his parents' grave when another heavy shadow sweeps across him giving him 'a bit of a start':

I looked over my shoulder. It was only a bombing plane which had flown between me and the sun.[44]

As he says, his is far from a Wordsworthian vision and in the

closing sentences of the chapter Bowling is to be found asserting a familiar doctrine: that man's moral salvation lies in his
freedom of personal contact with nature, of direct, unmediated experience, and that so long as he retains that he is safe
from subversion. When the boys get home from their expedi-
tion, the older ones seek to minimise George's success, so that
despite the 'tendency of fish, when people talk about
them, . . . to get bigger and bigger, . . . this one got smaller
and smaller'.

> But it didn't matter. I'd been fishing. I'd seen the float
> dive under the water and felt the fish tugging at the line,
> and however many lies they told they couldn't take that
> away from me.[45]

Here the 'they' is simply the rest of the gang, but standing in
this self-contained and terse little paragraph the pronoun has
a sinister suggestiveness which troublingly evokes those
powers that seek to prise the individual away from his personal allegiance to his own sense-impressions, and which flit continuously in and out of this story.

The book is always doing this sort of thing; moving out from
the highly particularised experience of the past, via the
thoroughly identifiable sensibility of Bowling at forty-five, to a
threatening future. What Bowling records is not physical
change primarily but rather a cultural and moral one. His
reverence is not for the past simply because it is the past nor
for the objects and experiences of that time simply because
they recall a lost youth, but because the past in its fixity and
accessibility will allow the individual the means to define himself for himself. It is a back-up system for those objects and experiences of that time ensuring their continuing vitality as
points of moral reference, and so enabling him once again in
the smell of latakia and sainfoin to get in touch with the proof
of his individuality. Even a capacity and freedom to savour
sounds and smells can be seen as vital anti-totalitarian equipment and he takes an image from nature (by no means at its
most attractive) and juxtaposes it with an inorganic one to
drive home the significance of his point:

> When I think of mother's kitchen . . . I always seem to hear

the bluebottles buzzing and smell the dustbin, and also old Nailer, who carried a pretty powerful smell of dog. And God knows there are worse smells and sounds. Which would you sooner listen to, a bluebottle or a bombing plane?[46]

When he concludes one of his reviews of the past with, 'Is it gone for ever? I'm not certain. But I tell you it was a good world to live in. I belong to it. So do you',[42] he is asserting a fundamental individualist position that all men seen and valued in what he has been considering as this Protestant light belong to the past. But he has no confidence that such a position will be maintained – quite the contrary; which is why he is allowing himself a little sentimental indulgence over his childhood. It is not, he points out, 'my own particular childhood, but the civilisation which I grew up in and which is now, I suppose, just about at its last kick'.[48] What he is witnessing, it seems to him, is an enormous cultural shift, when the old assumptions about humanity, the old moral values based upon the idea of an individual self are sinking under the onslaught of dark, uncompromising, absolutist powers:

> It's easy enough to die if the things you care about are going to survive. You've had your life, you're getting tired, it's time to go underground – that's how people used to see it. Individually they were finished, but their way of life would continue. Their good and evil would remain good and evil. They didn't feel the ground they stood on shifting under their feet.[49]

At the same time, no remark could express better than that first sentence the true combative, sectarian spirit.

George Bowling is as oppressed by the totalitarian threat as Orwell had been *Homage to Catalonia* and just as Orwell's description there had been in itself a credal statement, so does Bowling's need and capacity to communicate his experience to himself and to us betray the same pressure. It is this which explains the urgency with which he seeks to transmit his experience and to gain our understanding. He is in fact offering us himself:

> I know, of course, that you think I'm exaggerating about

the size of those fish. You think, probably, that they were just medium-sized fish (a foot long, say) and that they've swollen gradually in my memory. But it isn't so. People tell lies about the fish they've caught and still more about the fish that are hooked and get away, but I never caught any of these or even tried to catch them, and I've no motive for lying. I tell you they were enormous.[50]

This passage shows how easy it is to underestimate *Coming Up for Air*. In Bowling's half-embarrassed earnestness there is, simultaneously, an awareness of the far from uncommon nature of his description and a stubborn determination to convey to us his impression in its intensity and reality. The effect is the proper novelistic one: that we, the readers, go a stage further and explicitly recognise the *moral* significance of this particular act of description.

But if this novel throws back to *Homage to Catalonia* it also throws forward to *Nineteen Eighty-Four*; and not least in Bowling's desire to find a sympathetic and consolatory environment in which he would understand more, and, of greater importance, be understood:

> But what really got me down was the kind of mental squalor, the kind of mental atmosphere in which the real reason why I'd gone to Lower Binfield wouldn't even be conceivable. That was what chiefly struck me at the moment. If I spent a week explaining to Hilda *why* I'd been to Lower Binfield she'd never understand. And who *would* understand, here in Ellesmere Road? Gosh! did I even understand myself?[51]

Lower Binfield is not so much a place as a moral absolute – though an absolute under which the ground is shifting. His appeal is consequently to be understood in his individualism – for comprehension of a sort that will allow him his wholeness without isolation. Naturally the ghastly Hilda hasn't the least conception of such a dimension and wife though she is can offer Bowling no understanding. A writer who *would* have understood, made this entry in his diary summarising Bowling's problem very succinctly:

Insignificant as I may be, nevertheless there is no one here

who understands me in my entirety. To have someone possessed of such understanding, a wife perhaps, would mean
to have support from every side, to have God.[52]

Bowlings desire is very like Kafka's as the latter puts it here. It
is of course Orwell's desire too: and the appeal *is* really for
God. In *Nineteen Eighty-Four* O'Brien will answer the appeal,
his 'heavy, lined face, so ugly and so intelligent' compelling
Winston Smith to the realisation that 'one does not want to be
loved so much as to be understood'. Orwell's search for the
face that will show understanding and, perhaps, compassion
can be seen as yet another product of that complex and subtle
interplay of initiative and guilt so characteristic both of his
own moral response and of that Western religious movement
with which it is organically connected. Very aware of his duty
to his own conscience and his need to remain independent, he
nevertheless shows a remarkable yearning to unite with the
image of a wisdom large enough to contain all his contradictions, and powerful – and stern – enough to resolve them. The
defiance that Orwell had found in Dickens's face was very largely his own –

> It is the face of a man who is always fighting against some-
> thing, but who fights in the open and is not frightened, the
> face of a man who is *generously angry* – in other words, of a
> nineteenth century liberal, a free intelligence . . .

– but it was a defiance which, based on a constant refer-
ence-back to individual conscience, led increasingly to a sense
of isolation and insufficiency. Another face is sought: one
which will understand him and his weakness and ultimately
forgive and assimilate him. Erik Erikson talking of the dim
nostalgias which man may perceive when looking through a
glass darkly postulates at the centre of one of these nostalgias,

> the paternal voice of guiding conscience, which puts an end
> to the simple paradise of childhood and provides a sanction
> for energetic action. It also warns of the inevitability of
> guilty entanglement *and* threatens with the lightning of
> wrath. To change the threatening sound of this voice, if
> needs be by partial surrender and manifold self-castration,

is the second imperative demand which enters religious endeavour. At all cost the Godhead must be forced to indicate that He Himself mercifully planned crime and punishment in order to assure salvation.[53]

Though the language of this account may be a little specialised the spiritual model it describes is instantly recognisable as applicable to Orwell.

It is, of course, O'Brien who provides the most interesting (because the most developed) focus for this quest for the face which inspires fear or awe and yet offers hope of succour and absolution; but the Italian militiaman in *Homage to Catalonia* and, more particularly, the ex officer in *Coming Up for Air* who gives Bowling his chance in life, both exhibit the same charisma:

> He looked me up and down for a second. The two train-bearers had kind of wafted themselves a little distance away. I saw his rather good-looking old face, with the heavy grey eyebrows and the intelligent nose, looking me over and realized that he'd decided to help me. It's queer, the power of these rich men.[54]

For Winston, being understood by O'Brien is to be destroyed by him as an individual and Bowling too is very well aware that those who would seek to prevent his flight to Lower Binfield are made up of the uncomprehending who wouldn't understand, and the sinister who understood his reasons perfectly:

> . . . I was no sooner on the Oxford road than I felt perfectly certain that *they* knew all about it . . .
>
> What was more, I actually had a feeling that they were after me already. The whole lot of them! All the people who couldn't understand why a middle-aged man with false teeth should sneak away for a quiet week in the place where he spent his boyhood. And all the mean-minded bastards who *could* understand only too well, and who'd raise heaven and earth to prevent it. They were all on my track. It was as if a huge army were streaming up the road behind me.[55]

There are other more immediately obvious foretastes of *Nineteen Eighty-Four* in the references to 'the world we're going down into, the kind of hate-world, slogan-world' with its 'secret cells where the electric light burns night and day'. But it is in the fears and desires just discussed that *Coming Up for Air* offers the most seminal comparison, as we shall see when we look at the book where the individual is finally prised loose from his anchorage in nature and history, and his need to be understood transcends everything else.

7 Extra Ecclesiam Nulla Salus

Whom wilt thou find to love ignoble thee, Save Me, save
only Me?

Francis Thompson

. . . the deepest search in life, it seemed to me, the thing
that in one way or another was central to all living was
man's search to find a father, not merely the father of his
flesh, not merely the lost father of his youth, but the
image of a strength and wisdom external to his need and
superior to his hunger, to which the belief and power of
his own life could be united.

Thomas Wolfe

The dualism inaugurated by Luther, Machiavelli and
Descartes has brought us to the end of our tether and we
know that either we must discover a unity which can
repair the fissures that separate the individual from
society, feeling from intellect, and conscience from both,
or we shall surely die by spiritual despair and physical
annihilation.

W. H. Auden

Writing of George Orwell's feelings of guilt, George Woodcock concludes in *The Crystal Spirit* that it was inevitable that
he should begin to think of renunciation – 'even if it does not
take on a religious colouring'.[1] Lionel Trilling has claimed,
too, that 'although Orwell admired some of the effects and
attitudes of religion, he seems to have had no religious tendency in his nature, or none that went beyond what used to be
called natural piety.'[2] But Orwell's mind, as we have seen, is
deeply inbued with a 'religious colouring' and unless this is
recognised we can hardly avoid mistaking the fundamental
source of his guilt.

Of course Orwell had no belief in the existence of a deity, stopping short of confessed atheism only because of his dislike of systems and atheists. He has committed himself to an empirical individualism where man's moral and spiritual integrity, historically authenticated, depends on the basic freedom of a direct confrontation between the individual and the data of his experience, and on his sustaining his place in 'the stream of history'. For his own good he is clamped to 'objective reality.' But the strength this demands of the individual is enormous and the temptation is strong to return at whatever price into that larger identity from which, in the heresy of individualism, he has alienated himself. This temptation manifests itself in most, if not all, of Orwell's books but most powerfully in the unequal conflict between Winston Smith and the absolute and authoritarian Party in *Nineteen Eighty-Four*, where the nostalgic mirage of the Golden Country, as it is called there, ('A landscape I've seen sometimes in a dream'), is the last illusory reflection of the Golden City.

When Martin Luther declined to allow the Pope authority to interpret scripture on his behalf so that he might safeguard his spiritual integrity, he was searching for a credal wholeness through a kind of individual empiricism. In his own modest way – I have been making the comparison to establish the kind and not the degree of religious colouring – Orwell takes the same road and goes further along it, internalising God completely and taking as his principal scripture the book of nature. Both the affirmation and the drive behind it were very similar, reflecting a profound faith in the spiritual sanctity of the light within. But he no more than Luther escapes the consequences of his apostasy. Alongside his empiricism and independence runs not only guilt and a strong consciousness of the burden of his individuality, but also a fascination with the prospect of handing the responsibility over to some corporate care.

Disregarding *Nineteen Eighty-Four* as evidence, one could surmise that, in the last instance, Orwell would have agreed with Milton that one's religion was not 'a dividual movable'. But much more than Milton he would have been tempted to yield up that burden had the mediaeval church been around to receive it. As it was, his imagination provided an alternative.

To leave no doubt about the place of *Nineteen Eighty-Four* in the moral and ideological pattern that has been described, nor about the self-consistency of that pattern in its development, I would like to recall two of Orwell's statements already mentioned. The first is from his letter to Henry Miller when he confessed to having 'a sort of belly-to earth attitude' always feeling uneasy when he was 'away from the ordinary world where grass is green, stones hard, etc.'. Despite the casualness, the loyalties being confirmed here are fundamental to Orwell's moral vision. The greatest danger he can envisage for man (apart from being deprived of the means of historical self orientation) is that he should be denied such contact which allows him to measure and verify reality through what he sees as ultimately the only reliable medium, the evidence of the individual's senses.

If there is no reality verifiable by the senses, it is difficult to disprove that everything happens in the mind. And Orwell has little confidence in the individual mind holding out without such a fixed point against the determined assault of those who combine genius with the will to power. (O'Brien, we might recall, conspicuously manifests both: he is intelligent to the point of omniscience, able even to know what Winston is thinking, and he explicitly enunciates the doctrine 'God is Power'.) This distrust of 'pure' mind has a great deal to do with Orwell's fear of and for the intellectual. Winston Smith – and here it is possible I think to see him as an *alter ego* to Orwell – was oppressed above all 'with the consciousness of his own intellectual inferiority' in argument with O'Brien; with the 'thought of the unanswerable, mad arguments with which O'Brien would demolish him'.[3]

To permit the infringement of the individual's right to act on the evidence of his sense, or to allow the violation of the natural laws or to deny objective reality, was to take the first step towards subservience to the totalitarian: the natural laws, as Auden said, are of the divine. To recapitulate again:

> The atom bombs are piling up in the factories, the police are prowling through the cities, the lies are streaming from the loudspeakers, but the earth is still going round the sun,

and neither the dictators nor the bureaucrats deeply as they disapprove of the process are able to prevent it.

In *Nineteen Eighty-Four*, however, the dictators *do* prevent it, and it symbolises their absolute victory and control over the minds of men. But even here we might begin to question just who these dictators are and where they reside.

Enough has, I think, been said in previous chapters for us to see how deep are the origins of Orwell's brilliant understanding and portrayal of the psychology of totalitarianism. Sufficient, at any rate, to prevent our mistaking political insight for the matrix of his vision in *Nineteen Eighty-Four*. Only in a very superficial sense is this book talking about politics; for it is here that those drives and problems of the religious mind – of a very particular caste – clearly identified already, are most fully integrated in the creative process, finding at last an effective metaphorical form. That *Nineteen Eighty-Four* is, in fact, metaphorical should be beyond doubt and one is all the more surprised to find Professor Hodgart recently denying it:

> It is fashionable for literary critics to say that Utopian and anti-Utopian novels are not meant to be predictions, but are metaphors of the present state of society or of the permanent human situation. But this won't quite do for Orwell, who was almost naïvely interested in guessing what was going to happen. . . .

On the contrary, this *will* do for Orwell; or certainly the serious part of him. We are utterly mistaken if we persist in seeing this novel as a fiction of political science to be judged, as Professor Hodgart suggests, 'on whether or not the world is going the way it foretells'; a judgement which 'as we get nearer to the actual date of 1984 . . . becomes a little easier'.[4] (But what if we *don't* have telescreens in every room in the house in 1985?)

As *Nineteen Eighty-Four* makes abundantly clear and his other writing substantiates, Orwell's vision is the product of centuries of dialogue between the body and the soul, between man and his God. For him, as we have seen in all those references to a shift in consciousness 'three or four hundred years ago', the dialogue begins somewhere about the middle of the sixteenth century, though he views it, of course, with the enhanced perspective afforded by the accumulation of four hundred years. He is speaking in 'the present moment of the past' as Eliot called it. The inheritor of Luther, his preoccupation is with the sanctity and independence of the individual, but what he sees from his perspective is the wheel coming full circle and the individual sinking again, helpless and dependent, into total subservience to absolute authority. A process of denial and alienation has led inexorably to the point where re-admission to the abandoned whole is desired but available only at the price of a more complete self-abnegation even than before. For Orwell the stages of man's progress are almost diagrammatically clear. From dependence and reliance on infallible Papal authority transmitted by the Church the individual was 'rescued' by Luther, the personal contract with God established and with it the paramount importance of personal responsibility: this is the first stage, the denial of the Pope and his Church. Then, in more modern times, comes the dereliction of faith in immortality, in absolute sanction for right and wrong, leaving the individual to defend his integrity as best he could ('This demands faith which is a different thing from credulity') with the help of 'nature', objective reality: the second stage, the denial of God. Finally and inevitably with the destruction of man's link with 'nature' through the medium of his senses comes the denial of the individual's independence and, once again, his submission:

> Alone – free – the human being is always defeated. It must be so, because every human being is doomed to die, which is the greatest of all failures. But if he can make complete, utter submission, if he can escape from his identity, if he can merge himself in the Party so that he *is* the Party, then he is all-powerful and immortal.[5]

Nineteen Eighty-Four describes the last stages of the process: the hopeless struggle of a man to retain his grip on empirical reality and so on his individuality. Much like Orwell, Winston Smith has discovered that the latter depends on his right and capacity to believe that 'Stones are hard, water is wet, objects unsupported fall towards the earth's centre'. With the feeling 'that he was setting forth an important axiom' he writes in his forbidden diary:

> Freedom is the freedom to say that two plus two make four. If that is granted, all else follows.[6]

It is O'Brien's job to convince him of the deformity of his vision and win him back to the Party:

> You believe that reality is something objective, external, existing in its own right. You also believe that the nature of reality is self-evident. When you delude yourself into thinking that you see something, you assume that everyone else sees the same thing as you. But I tell you, Winston, that reality is not external. Reality exists in the human mind, and nowhere else. Not in the individual mind, which can make mistakes, and in any case soon perishes: only in the mind of the Party, which is collective and immortal. Whatever the Party holds to be truth, *is* truth. It is impossible to see reality except by looking through the eyes of the Party. That is the fact that you have got to relearn, Winston. It needs an act of self-destruction, an effort of the will. You must humble yourself before you can become sane.* [7]

But Winston is aware that once his hold on the external world is loosened, once he has been alienated from his own sense-impressions, he is morally adrift and totally at the mercy of the superior intelligence and the will to power. So he recognises the objective in the Party's determination to make reality totally fluid by falsifying the records and destroying the past as a point of reference, thus isolating man from that accumulated body of human experience which is both proof and sum of the autonomous individual, and enabling the Party to create him anew. Lies become truths overnight with the help of the Records Department, and the essential mental quality required by the Party is Doublethink:

> *Doublethink* means the power of holding two contradictory beliefs in one's mind simultaneously, and accepting both of them. The Party intellectual knows in which direction his

---

* It is worthwhile underlining how much of O'Brien's argument is a rebuttal of that large part of Orwell's own moral system which was based, as we have seen, on an attachment to 'objective reality' and faith in the evidence of one's senses.

memories must be altered; he therefore knows that he is playing tricks with reality; but by the exercise of *doublethink* he also satisfies himself that reality is not violated. The process has to be conscious, or it would not be carried out with sufficient precision, but it also has to be unconscious, or it would bring with it a feeling of falsity and hence of guilt. *Doublethink* lies at the very heart of Ingsoc, since the essential act of the Party is to use conscious deception while retaining the firmness of purpose that goes with complete honesty. To tell deliberate lies while genuinely believing in them, to forget any fact that has become inconvenient, and then, when it becomes necessary again, to draw it back from oblivion for just so long as it is needed, to deny the existence of objective reality and all the while to take account of the reality which one denies – all this is indispensably necessary.[8]

From which one might conclude rudely that the only possible manipulator of *doublethink* would be God himself. To live in this contradiction the individual has to be no more than a shell to be filled up with whatever response is required; but for O'Brien, for example, to live it and to manipulate it is to comprehend and therefore transcend the antinomy and postulate Absolute Mind.

The empty shell is of course exactly what the Party is aiming for and it is in these terms that O'Brien describes the 'processing' of its victims:

No one whom we bring to this place ever stands out against us. Everyone is washed clean. Even those three miserable traitors in whose innocence you once believed – Jones, Aaronson, and Rutherford – in the end we broke them down. I took part in their interrogation myself. I saw them gradually worn down, whimpering, grovelling, weeping – and in the end it was not with pain or fear, only with penitence. By the time we had finished with them they were only the shells of men. There was nothing left in them except sorrow for what they had done, and love of Big Brother. It was touching to see how they loved him. They begged to be shot quickly, so that they could die while their minds were still clean.[9]

Winston himself is assured in an appropriately religious idiom
that after his treatment he, too, will be 'hollow': 'We shall
squeeze you empty and then we shall fill you with ourselves'.[10]

From the start Winston had realised that his own creed –
his insistence on the moral need for the individual to confront
experience directly and act on the basis of his *own* interpretation – was the rankest heresy to the absolutist creed of
the Party. (The book in the following quotation is, we might
note, also a *history* book.)

> He picked up the children's history book and looked at the
> portrait of Big Brother which formed its frontispiece. The
> hypnotic eyes gazed into his own. It was as though some
> huge force were pressing down upon you – something that
> penetrated inside your skull, battering against your brain,
> frightening you out of your beliefs, persuading you, almost,
> to deny the evidence of your senses. In the end the Party
> would announce that two and two made five, and you
> would have to believe it. It was inevitable that they should
> make that claim sooner or later: the logic of their position
> demanded it. Not merely the validity of experience, but the
> very existence of external reality, was tacitly denied by their
> philosophy.[11]

And Orwell's choice of language is surely a significant pointer
to the moral structure he is invoking when Winston concludes
that 'the heresy of heresies was common sense'. It is a heresy
for which, in the traditional manner, he will be tortured and
condemned.

The battle is not between democracy and totalitarianism,
except as a paradigm: it is between on the one hand, the age-
old human need for the individual to find his own meaning to
the universe, his own salvation, and so to fulfil those incom-
municable depths of self, and, on the other, an absolutist
authoritarianism determined that such freedom should
remain undistributed and that its control over the individual
should be absolute. The final and even shocking irony,
however, comes with the revelation that this battle-ground has
yet another dimension where the ambition in the soul for
autonomy is seen to be contending with its own nostalgia for

re-assimilation in an all-consuming Identity.

To ensure success the Party first dislocates the individual from objective reality, but this is only the initial stage which makes the total moral evisceration of the individual easier to achieve. Family relations must also be broken down, so children are encouraged to spy on their parents. (It is Parsons' children who betray him to the Thought-Police.) Of no less a threat to the Party is the relationship between Winston and Julia. John Osborne's Luther, also fighting for an empirical independence, had recognised this truth by putting such relationships very high in his scheme of values:

> Seems to me there are three ways out of despair. One is faith in Christ, the second is to become enraged by the world and make its nose bleed for it, and the third is the love of a woman.[12]

The love between Julia and Winston is as exalted morally as 'Luther's' claim for it here, for it enshrines the fast-fading reality of private standards and impulses, of personal feelings and an interior world of soul:

> 'Confession is not betrayal. What you say or do doesn't matter: only feelings matter. If they could make me stop loving you – that would be the real betrayal.'
>
> She thought it over. 'They can't do that', she said finally. 'It's the one thing they can't do. They can make you say anything – *anything* – but they can't make you believe it. They can't get inside you.'
>
> 'No,' he said a little more hopefully, 'no; that's quite true. They can't get inside you. If you can *feel* that staying human is worthwhile, even when it can't have any result whatever, you've beaten them.'[13]

Nostalgically Winston evokes a Bloomsbury-world where personal relationships and personal feelings were what conferred dignity and reality on the individual. He remembers his mother:

> He did not suppose, from what he could remember of her, that she had been an unusual woman, still less an intelligent one; and yet she had possessed a kind of nobility, a

kind of purity, simply because the standards that she obeyed were private ones. Her feelings were her own, and could not be altered from outside. It would not have occurred to her that an action which is ineffectual thereby becomes meaningless. If you loved someone, you loved him, and when you had nothing else to give, you still gave him love. When the last of the chocolate was gone, his mother had clasped the child in her arms. It was no use, it changed nothing, it did not produce more chocolate, it did not avert the child's death or her own; but it seemed natural to her to do it.[14]

There is much emphasis in the novel on wordless gesture as the last vestigial remnants of that vanishing interior life full of private meaning. Winston, for example, is haunted by the image of the woman in the film he had seen raising her arm in a futile attempt to protect the child against machine-gun bullets. In the dream he has – a dream that is half-memory – while sleeping with Julia in the room above Mr. Charrington's shop, this woman merges with his mother into a symbol of maternal love, and something more. When Winston as a small boy at the time of the revolution had snatched the last piece of chocolate from his sister lying in his mother's arms, his mother 'drew her arm round the child and pressed it to her breast. Something in the gesture told him that his sister was dying.' Now Winston feels that his dream 'in which his whole life seemed to stretch out before him like a landscape on a summer evening after rain' had been, as he says,

> comprehended by – indeed, in some sense it had consisted in – a gesture of the arm made by his mother, and made again thirty years later by the Jewish woman he had seen on the news film trying to shelter the small boy from the bullets, before the helicopter blew them both to pieces.[15]

Thus the maternal 'curve' or gesture becomes the enclosing round which had defined the private, internal world of personal feelings and as such it is beautifully extended visually and metaphorically in the dome of the glass paperweight. For the paperweight is itself the emblem of that ideal of a private, individual existence which Winston knows to be doomed. Lying in bed gazing on it Winston sees it encapsulating his life and Julia's:

> The inexhaustibly interesting thing was not the fragment of coral but the interior of the glass itself. There was such a depth in it, and yet it was almost as transparent as air. It was as though the surface of the glass had been the arch of the sky, enclosing a tiny world with its atmosphere complete. He had the feeling that he could get inside it, and that in fact he was inside it, along with the mahogany bed and the gateleg table, and the clock and the steel engraving and the paperweight itself. The paperweight was the room he was in, and the coral was Julia's life and his own, fixed in a sort of eternity at the heart of the crystal.[16]

Winston himself links the paperweight and the personal gesture, for his dream had not only been 'comprehended' by the gesture of an arm, he felt that it had

> 'all occurred inside the glass paperweight, but the surface of the glass was the dome of the sky, and inside the dome everything was flooded with clear soft light in which one could see interminable distances'.[17]

Developing the figure of the paperweight, Orwell secures a devastating effect and an utterly conclusive destruction of the world it signifies when what Winston has described as 'a little chunk of history that they've forgotten to alter' (in its evocative summary of that mysterious, personal world) is pulverised by the secret police who finally invade their sanctum:

> There was another crash. Someone had picked up the glass paperweight from the table and smashed it to pieces on the hearth-stone.
>
> The fragment of coral, a tiny crinkle of pink like a sugar rose-bud from a cake, rolled across the mat. How small, thought Winston, how small it always was.[18]

In calculated opposition to the spirit implicit in the gesture of the woman in the film, the Party had set out to pursuade people 'that mere impulses, mere feelings, were of no account, while at the same time robbing [them] of all power over the material world.'[19] The inquisitor in Schiller's Don Carlos described accurately the Party's position from what might be called a sympathetic point of view (in sharp contrast to 'Luther's' evaluation of human relationship):

> *The King* (contemplating murdering his son): I outrage nature. Wouldst thou also stifle that mighty voice?
>
> *Inquisitor*: It is of no account the voice of nature, weighed against our faith.

O'Brien's attitude is a very similar one and Orwell is aware of it:

> You have heard of the religious persecution of the past. In the Middle Ages there was the Inquisition. It was a failure. It set out to eradicate heresy and ended by perpetuating it.[20]

The difference between the two is very largely technological. O'Brien habitually speaks from the same text often using the same religious vocabulary:

> Your name was removed from the registers, every record of discipline. You would not make the act of submission which is the price of sanity. You preferred to be a lunatic, a minority of one. Only the disciplined mind can see reality, Winston.[21]

The authority he asserts over the individual is absolute. Opposition results in total erasure as Winston reminds himself when he starts his diary:

> You name was removed from the registers, every record of everything you had ever done was wiped out, your one-time existence was denied and then forgotten. You were abolished, annihilated: *vaporized* was the usual word.[22]

Being 'lifted clean out of the stream of history' is the logical end for anyone who, in the name of his individuality, challenges the absolutist creed of the Party. Winston expects annihilation and it is what O'Brien promises him:

> You must stop imagining that posterity will vindicate you, Winston. Posterity will never hear of you. You will be lifted

clean out from the stream of history. We shall turn you into gas and pour you into the stratosphere. Nothing will remain of you; not a name in a register, not a memory in a living brain. You will be annihilated in the past as well as in the future. You will never have existed.[23]

Despite the trimmings, this is still the language of the mediaeval church dealing with its heretics as von der Eck's words quoted at the very beginning of this study testify; and inevitably so, for the issues are the same still:

. . . if you alter your views [The Emperor] will prevail upon the supreme pontiff not to destroy and blot out the good with the bad. If, however you obstinately persist in your notorious errors and heresies as up to the present, most certainly all memory of you will be wiped out, and everything, whether right or wrong, together with their author, will be condemned.

Virtually everything about the Party, its structure and its creed, invite comparison with the mediaeval church, and, as suggested already, Orwell shows himself aware of it. It is not insignificant that the only other historical period admitted by the Party is the Middle Ages:

Anything large and impressive, if it was reasonably new in appearance, was automatically claimed as having been built since the Revolution, while anything that was obviously of earlier date was ascribed to some dim period called the Middle Ages. The centuries of capitalism were held to have produced nothing of any value.[24]

The centuries of capitalism being also the centuries of Protestant individualism. The comparison is made direct in 'the book' which offers a critique of the new system:

[The older kind of Socialist] did not see that the continuity of an oligarchy need not be physical, nor did he pause to reflect that hereditary aristocracies have always been short-lived, whereas adoptive organizations such as the Catholic Church have sometimes lasted for hundreds or thousands of years. The essence of oligarchical rule is not father-to-son inheritance, but the persistence of a certain world-view and a certain way of life, imposed by the dead upon the living. A ruling group is a ruling group so long as it can nominate its successors. The Party is not concerned with perpetuating its blood but with perpetuating itself. *Who* wields power is not important, provided that the hierarchical structure remains always the same.[25]

And the two are constantly being drawn together in such comparisons as 'Even the Catholic Church of the Middle Ages was tolerant by modern standards'.[26]

When Winston, still recalcitrant even under torture, disputes O'Brien's claim that the Party's control over matter is absolute –

'But how can you control matter? . . . You don't even control the climate or the law of gravity . . .'

– he is silenced by O'Brien's reply that they control all these because they control the mind:

There is nothing that we could not do. Invisibility, levitation – anything. I could float off this floor like a soap bubble if I wish to. I do not wish to, because the Party does not wish it. You must get rid of those nineteenth-century ideas about the laws of Nature. We make the laws of Nature.

And when in response to O'Brien's flat statement that 'outside man there is nothing' Winston argues

'But the whole universe is outside us. Look at the stars! Some of them are a million light-years away. They are out of our reach forever'

he is met with an answer which would have been all too familiar in its essence and inspiration to a Bruno or a Galileo:

'What are the stars?' said O'Brien indifferently. 'They are bits of fire a few kilometres away. We could reach them if we wanted to. Or we could blot them out. The earth is the centre of the universe. The sun and the stars go round it.'[27]

Indeed, with the (willed) obscurantism of 'they are bits of fire' we *are* back in the middle ages.

All this is in addition to the more obvious overtones in reference to the Party being 'in possession of absolute truth' or to the mind of the Party being 'collective and immortal'.

Then there is the identity suggested in the Party's very clearly theological hierarchy:

> At the apex of the pyramid comes Big Brother. Big Brother is infallible and all-powerful. Every success, every achievement, every victory, every scientific discovery, all knowledge, all wisdom, all happiness, all virtue, are held to issue directly from his leadership and inspiration. Nobody has ever seen Big Brother. He is a face on the hoardings, a voice on the telescreen. We may be reasonably sure that he will never die, and there is already considerable uncertainty as to when he was born. Big Brother is the guise in which the Party chooses to exhibit itself to the world. His function is to act as a focusing point for love, fear, and reverence, emotions which are more easily felt towards an individual than towards an organization.[28]

Even without this particular quotation in mind we find nothing incongruous in the behaviour of the devout lady-member described during the routine 'office' of the Two Minutes Hate (itself a sort of perverted communion)*:

> With a tremulous murmur that sounded like 'My Saviour! she extended her arms towards the screen. Then she buried her face in her hands. It was apparent that she was uttering a prayer.[29]

Elsewhere we hear frequently of Big Brother's divinity:

> Oceanic society rests ultimately on the belief that Big Brother is omnipotent and that the Party is infallible.[31]

Indeed the Party generally plays Pope to his God.

> ... by far the more important reason for the readjustment of the past is the need to safeguard the infallibility of the Party. It is not merely that speeches, statistics, and records

* We might note, incidentally, another communion ritual, though this time a dissenting one, when O'Brien, Julia and Winston take wine together. It ends, ironically, with Julia being given 'a flat white tablet . . . to place on her tongue' – to kill the smell of the wine.[30]

of every kind must be constantly brought up to date in order to show that the predictions of the Party were in all cases right. It is also that no change in doctrine or in political alignment can ever be admitted. For to change one's mind, or even one's policy, is a confession of weakness.[32]

The role of the Inner Party then follows naturally: 'We are the priests of Power', says O'Brien, 'God is Power'.[33]

For most of the time O'Brien plays the role of Cardinal Inquisitor, if not actually of the Pope himself.* Thus the confrontation between him and Winston is an extreme one. He is not a Parsons or a Symes, he is the system just as Winston is its antithesis. And in his inquisitorial role he performs in the most traditional manner, seeking out the sins of heretics in order to win back their souls. The whole emphasis in the latter part of *Nineteen Eighty-Four*, so often misunderstood, is not on punishment but on conversion. This is why it is so prolonged.

As for Winston, his performance is a remarkable confirmation of O'Brien in his role by being so perfectly that of the heretic in its mixture of defiance, doubt, guilt and yearning for absolution. He shows himself tormented by his own individuality, wholly pessimistic about the individual's capacity to hold out, uncertain, even, if it is right for him to try to do so. It is the fullest expression of that classic Lutheran anxiety which figures so prominently throughout Orwell's work: of an integrity-crisis which, as Erikson says, though 'last in the lives of ordinary men, is a life-long and chronic crisis in a *homo religiosus*'.[34]

From the start Winston feels himself doomed; and the start is significantly not a physical act but one of mental apostasy; a fall from grace:

> He had committed – would still have committed, even if he had never set pen to paper – the essential crime that contained all others in itself. Thought-crime, they called it.[35]

The repeated references to the certainty of detection and punishment (and we might recall here how this appeared in *Down and Out in Paris and London* and *The Road to Wigan Pier*) reveal the strength of his sense of guilt. In his rebellion the inevit-

---

* It may not be over-ingenious to see Catholicism implicit in the name O'Brien.

ability of his destruction is almost willed. ('In this game that we're playing, we can't win'.[36]) His sinfulness is inescapable and the one hope is that 'at an uncertain (and maybe immediately impending) moment, an end would come which might guarantee an individual the chance (to be denied to millions of others) of finding pity before the only true Identity, the only true Reality, which was Divine Wrath'* :

> Both of them knew – in a way, it was never out of their minds – that what was now happening could not last long. There were times when the fact of impending death seemed as palpable as the bed they lay on, and they would cling together with a sort of despairing sensuality, like a damned soul grasping at his last morsel of pleasure when the clock is within five minutes of striking.[37]

And the phrase 'We are the dead' is reiterated several times almost as a ritual invocation until it finally secures the response from the telescreen behind the picture, 'You are the dead'.

There is, in fact, an ambiguity familiar to the heretical consciousness in what Winston does. He rebels in the name of his individuality but ultimately he has no enduring faith in the individual, and the suspicion grows that he rebels in order to be 'washed clean', annihilated and absorbed. If this were not the case there would be no explanation for his accepting, at the same time as he asserts free individual will, a relentless determinism that will ensure his destruction (the seeds of that destruction are, we note, mysteriously part of his nature – his first step had been an *involuntary* act):

> He knew that sooner or later he would obey O'Brien's summons. Perhaps to-morrow, perhaps after a long delay – he was not certain. What was happening was only the working-out of a process that had started years ago. The first step had been a secret, involuntary thought, the second had been the opening of the diary. He had moved from thoughts to words, and now from words to actions. The last step was something that would happen in the Ministry of Love. He

---

* These words are Erik Erikson's speculative interpretation of the world-image of man which may have suggested itself to the young Martin Luther. See *Young Man Luther*, p 72.

had accepted it. The end was contained in the beginning. But it was frightening: or, more exactly, it was like a fore-taste of death, like being a little less alive. Even while he was speaking to O'Brien, when the meaning of the words had sunk in, a chilly shuddering feeling had taken posses-sion of his body. He had the sensation of stepping into the dampness of a grave, and it was not much better because he had always known that the grave was there and waiting for him.[38]

The ambiguity is excellently conveyed in Winston's attitude to O'Brien, the Inquisitor. If he *really* believed that O'Brien was a fellow-conspirator, there would be no such ambiguity; but palpably he does not. Right at the beginning there is an extremely suggestive remark:

[Winston] felt deeply drawn to him, and not solely because he was intrigued by the contrast between O'Brien's urbane manner and his prize-fighter's physique. Much more it was because of a secretly-held belief – or perhaps not even a belief, merely a hope – that O'Brien's political orthodoxy was not perfect. Something in his face suggested it irresist-ibly. And again, perhaps it was not even unorthodoxy that was written in his face, but simply intelligence.[39]

The last sentence is of great significance: a significance which is made more explicit a little later:

Winston had never been able to feel sure – even after this morning's flash of the eyes it was still impossible to be sure – whether O'Brien was a friend or an enemy. Nor did it even seem to matter greatly. There was a link of under-standing between them, more important than affection or partisanship.[40]

When, finally, O'Brien confronts him as Party Chief and Inquisitor in the cell in the depths of the Ministry of Love he shows up Winston's self-deception for what it is:

'You knew this, Winston,' said O'Brien. 'Don't deceive yourself. You did know it – you have always known it.'*[41]

---

* It is worth comparing this and other references to Winston 'always having

What recommends O'Brien to him is his intelligence and omniscient understanding. For his confessional soul this was of the highest importance. Even without knowing for sure about O'Brien's unorthodoxy he has the strongest desire 'simply to walk into O'Brien's presence, announce that he was the enemy of the Party, and demand his help'.[42] Help to do what, we might ask, if he is not sure about O'Brien's unorthodoxy. His inclination to prostrate himself – 'A wave of admiration, almost of worship, flowed out from Winston towards O'Brien'[43] – leaves no room for doubt.

His desire is to be understood: to be received into that ambience where all contradictions and struggle will be resolved in a mind large enough to contain his:

> O'Brien was a being in all ways larger than himself. There was no idea that he had ever had, or could have, that O'Brien had not long ago known, examined, and rejected. His mind *contained* Winston's mind.[44]

So he delivers himself up to torture in search of the true identity, and O'Brien receives him, as one who must be saved.

> 'Don't worry, Winston; you are in my keeping . . . I shall save you, I shall make you perfect'.[45]

The torture is explicitly designed to purify:

> . . . we make the brain perfect before we blow it out . . . No one whom we bring to this place ever stands out against us. Everyone is washed clean.[46]

And there is no cruelty here. Winston *wants* to be saved and would see five fingers instead of the four if he could possibly transcend his sinful vision.

> 'You are a slow learner, Winston', said O'Brien gently. 'How can I help it?' he blubbered. 'How can I help seeing what is in front of my eyes? Two and two are four'. . . .
> 'How many fingers, Winston?'
> 'Four. I suppose there are four. I would see five if I could. I am trying to see five.'

---

known' with Gordon Comstock's frequent admissions of always having known about his latent self-betrayal.

'Which do you wish: to persuade me that you see five, or really to see them?'
'Really to see them.'[47]

Despite the torture, Winston still regards O'Brien as the source of salvation: the source of the pain he feels to be somewhere else, unconnected with Big Brother's Vicar-General to whom he can turn for relief and comfort:

> He had the feeling that O'Brien was his protector, that the pain was something that came from outside, from some other source, and that it was O'Brien who would save him from it.[48]

More than ever O'Brien appears as the Inquisitor, joined with the heretic in combat with the Devil. As such, he is not responsible for the pain: that lies in the evil at the root of Winston's sin. In other words the Devil they are fighting is individualism. The degree to which they are collaborators and the sincerity of Winston's desire to become part of the all-comprehending Identity is finally established beyond a doubt.

> He opened his eyes and looked up gratefully at O'Brien. At sight of the heavy, lined face, so ugly and so intelligent, his heart seemed to turn over. If he could have moved he would have stretched out a hand and laid it on O'Brien's arm. He had never loved him so deeply as at this moment, and not merely because he had stopped the pain. The old feeling, that at bottom it did not matter whether O'Brien was a friend or an enemy, had come back. O'Brien was a person who could be talked to. Perhaps one did not want to be loved so much as to be understood. O'Brien had tortured him to the edge of lunacy, and in a little while, it was certain, he would send him to his death. It made no difference. In some sense that went deeper than friendship, they were intimates: somewhere or other, although the actual words might never be spoken, there was a place where they could meet and talk.[49]

This final surrender to O'Brien is the culminating and revealing acknowledgement by Orwell of the depth of his response to the image of – and here we might use the words of Thomas

Wolfe quoted at the head of his chapter – 'a strength and wisdom external to his need and superior to his hunger, to which the belief and power of his own life could be united'. Of the fact that the acknowledgement *is* by Orwell and not just Winston Smith there can be little doubt by this time. It is not simply the obvious and superficial echoes of Orwell's personal temper and preoccupations which convince us of this: the word 'intimates', for example, in the last quotation recalling Orwell's desire to know people 'intimately' and his spirit's meeting with the militiaman's 'in utter intimacy'; or the fact that O'Brien, at the moment of surrender, revealingly brings together physical impressiveness earlier admired by the activist, and the intellectual power which Orwell had long regarded as a potentially sinister force likely to subvert the individual from his essential loyalties. These are ancillary pieces of evidence. As the rest of this study has shown unequivocally Orwell was haunted by a confessional need for the sort of image Wolfe describes. To show just how far it reached, however, one last and quite explicit reference may be allowed:

> [James Joyce] dared . . . to expose the imbecilities of the inner mind, and in doing so he discovered an America which was under everybody's nose . . . The effect is to break down, at any rate momentarily, the solitude in which the human being lives. When you read certain passages in *Ulysses* you feel that Joyce's mind and your mind are one, that he knows all about you though he has never heard your name, that there exists some world outside time and space in which you and he are together. And though he does not resemble Joyce in other ways, there is a touch of this quality in Henry Miller. . . . read him for five pages, ten pages, and you feel the peculiar relief that comes not so much from understanding as from *being understood*.[50]

The italics are Orwell's.

*   *   *

So the text so derided by Orwell in 'Inside the Whale' – Though He slay me yet will I trust in Him – comes to be Winston Smith's last testament. It is a text which by this time we recognise to be subsumed in a very great deal of Orwell's

writing: it is present, for example, in the pervasive appeal
which self-abnegation shows itself to exert and in Orwell's fascination with the role of victim. We can be in no doubt at all
about the abasement being, in the last analysis, voluntary. In
Nineteen Eighty-Four, as the foregoing argument makes clear,
the definitive change to submissive resignation from a by now
faltering empirical individualism – itself a sad regression from
those other occasions when it has declared itself ready to make
the world's nose bleed for it – is not ultimately wrought by the
Party, for the Party is not to be regarded, simply, as an external (only the pain 'came from outside'). What it does is to
offer a discipline and an identity, but it is Winston Smith who
needs these and has created them in this shape.

In Brecht's play *Galileo* Cardinal Barberini talking at the
masked ball with Galileo on the effects of the latter's dis-
coveries on such discipline and identity remarks:

> It is my mask that permits me a little freedom today . . . In
> such a get-up you might hear me murmuring: if there were
> no God one would have to invent one. Good, let us put up
> our masks again. Poor Galilei has none.

In the end Winston Smith gratefully accepts the mask the
Party offers, having had, like Galilei, none at the beginning.

Winston has created – or recreated – the Party and so
betrayed himself in his individualism. This is why *Nineteen
Eighty-Four* is a tragedy and so powerful. The struggle – all
along in the soul – has been to defend an autonomous moral
freedom against absolutism and assimilation in the larger
identity. But this last has exerted an irresistible fascination in
face of the pressures which the alternative creates, and the
battle for independence has been conceded.

Thus the terror of the sanctuary Winston finds in O'Brien is
the consciousness of his own betrayal. Now there are no
means left whereby he can escape the confrontation. Brutally
O'Brien compels him to face his own reflection in the mirror:
no longer can there be any refuge in disguise – as there had
once been for 'Orwell' in earlier works:

> 'Go on', said O'Brien. 'Stand between the wings of the
> mirror. You shall see the side view as well.'

He had stopped because he was frightened. A bowed, grey-coloured, skeleton-like thing was coming towards him. Its actual appearance was frightening, and not merely the fact that he knew it to be himself. . . . The creature's face seemed to be protruded, because of its bent carriage. A forlorn, jailbird's face with a nobby forehead running back into a bald scalp, a crooked nose, and battered-looking cheekbones . . . Except for his hands and a circle of his face, his body was grey all over with ancient, ingrained dirt. Here and there under the dirt there were the red scars of wounds, and near the ankle the varicose ulcer was an inflamed mass with flakes of skin peeling off it . . .

'You are rotting away', [O'Brien] said, 'You are falling to pieces. What are you? A bag of filth. Now turn round and look into that mirror again. Do you see that thing facing you? That is the last man. If you are human, that is humanity. Now put your clothes on again.'[51]

Like Gordon Comstock who had 'always known' that he would give up the struggle, Winston had, of course, 'always known' that he would be defeated – though he would never admit that it was what he wanted. He had 'always known' that O'Brien was of the Party – though he would never admit the knowledge. He had 'always known' what was behind the wall – though he would not admit it. ('In the dream his deepest feeling was always one of self-deception, because he did in fact know what was behind the wall of darkness'.[52]) In fact the rats, far from being the horror-film extras of some contemporary criticism – are a symbol and a part of his self-deception. He knows what they are but refuses to bring them out into the open: to do so would be to confront the knowledge of his own self-betrayal, as well as to pre-empt that moment of ultimate terror when the nameless fear he has refused to exorcise – 'with a deadly effort, like wrenching a piece out of his own brain, he could even have dragged the thing into the open' – finally extinguishes his heresy.

The betrayal was his own doing and so complete as to be utterly irrevocable. His cry of 'Do it to Julia' sums up everything. ('If they could make me stop loving you,' he had said,

'that would be the real betrayal.') It sums up his self-betrayal,
his complete loss of integrity, of ownership of his own feelings;
his aspersion of personal feeling, individuality and love:

'What happens to you here is *for ever*,' O'Brien had said.
That was a true word. There were things, your own acts,
from which you could not recover. Something was killed in
your breast; burnt out, cauterized out.[53]

But the heretic has his reward. Absolved, his *soul* white as
snow, he returns to the fold no longer a heretic but a prodigal
son loving his father and confident of the final dispensation:

Winston, sitting in a blissful dream, paid no attention as his
glass was filled up. He was not running or cheering any
longer. He was back in the Ministry of Love, with
everything forgiven, his soul white as snow. He was in the
public dock, confessing everything, implicating everybody.
He was walking down the white-tiled corridor, with the
feeling of walking in sunlight, and an armed guard at his
back. The long-hoped-for bullet was entering his brain.

He gazed up at the enormous face. Forty years it had
taken him to learn what kind of smile was hidden beneath
the dark moustache. O cruel, needless misunderstanding!
O stubborn, self-willed exile from the loving breast! Two
gin-scented tears trickled down the sides of his nose. But it
was all right, everything was all right, the struggle was finished. He had won the victory over himself. He loved Big
Brother.[54]

This is the large dimension of Orwell's tragic irony: individualism, the prized and fought for freedom, is betrayed by
itself. *Nineteen Eighty-Four* is a sad and bitter comment not
especially on 1984, but on the eclipse of that brave new world
which swam into view with Copernicus, Bruno, Luther and
Galileo, and was epitomised by the latter, as Brecht drama-
tised him, in these words:

Things are starting to move, Federzoni; we may yet live to
see the day when we no longer have to look over our shoulders like criminals when we say that twice two is four.

Notes

Since this essay has not followed the lines of 'traditional' Orwell scholarship I have not thought it necessary to subscribe a lengthy bibliography. Works on Orwell which have been referred to in the book will be found in the index. One book which does not appear there since it came to hand when this study was very near completion but which deserves to be mentioned, is Raymond Williams' short but excellent work in the Fontana Modern Masters series, *Orwell*. I am, of course, greatly indebted to *The Collected Essays, Journalism and Letters of George Orwell,* edited by Sonia Orwell and Ian Angus, and, in a different way, to Erik Erikson's admirable *Young Man Luther*.

In the notes overleaf references are to the Penguin edition of the following works, published in association with Secker & Warburg.

Down and Out in Paris and London (1969)
Burmese Days (1967)
A Clergyman's Daughter (1969)
Keep the Aspidistra Flying (1968)
The Road to Wigan Pier (1967)
Homage to Catalonia (1968)
Animal Farm (1972)
Nineteen Eighty-Four (1969)

In the notes *The Collected Essays, Journalism and Letters of George Orwell,* (Martin Secker and Warburg, 1968) has had the title abbreviated to *CEJL*

CHAPTER I

1. B.L. Woolf (trans.), *Reformation Writings of Martin Luther*, vol. 2 (London, 1956) p. 152.
2. Ibid., p. 155 (quoted from the anonymous version of the proceedings).
3. Erik Erikson, *Young Man Luther* (London, 1959) pp. 188, 189-90.
4. Irving Howe, 'The Fiction of Anti-Utopia', in *Orwell's Nineteen Eighty-Four: Text, Sources, Criticism.* (ed. Howe, New York, 1963) p. 178.

5. 'Literature and Totalitarianism', *CEJL*, *vol.* 2, 134.
6. 'The Prevention of Literature', in *CEJL*, *vol.* 4, 65.
7. Ibid., pp. 68-9.
8. 'Culture and Democracy' in *Victory and Vested Interest* (London, 1942) p. 93.

CHAPTER 2

1. 'Such, Such Were the Joys', *CEJL*, vol. 4, 344.
2. *Burmese Days*, pp. 54-5.
3. *CEJL*, *vol.* 1, 228.
4. 'Why I Write', *CEJL*, vol. 1, 6.
5. Erik Erikson, *Young Man Luther*, p. 186.
6. Quoted by Erikson, op. cit., pp. 186-7.
7. *Coming Up for Air*, p. 164.
8. 'What is Science', *CEJL*, vol. 4, 12.
9. *Nineteen Eighty-Four*, p. 156.
10. 'Some Thoughts on the Common Toad', *CEJL*, vol. 4, 144-5.
11. *CEJL*, vol. 1, 375-6.
12. W.H. Auden in *Modern Canterbury Pilgrims*, ed. James A. Pike (London, 1956) p. 42.
13. Erik Erikson, op cit., p. 207.
14. *Down and Out in Paris and London*, p. 50.
15. Ibid., p. 108.
16. Ibid., p. 67.
17. Ibid., pp. 70-71.
18. Ibid., p. 15.
19. Ibid., p. 67.
20. Ibid., p. 72.
21. Rudyard Kipling, 'The Phantom Rickshaw', in *Wee Willie Winkie*, (Sussex Edition), 1937, p. 135.
22. *The Road to Wigan Pier*, p. 5.
23. Ibid., p. 15.
24. Ibid., p. 35.
25. 'Looking Back on the Spanish War', *CEJL*, vol. 2, 258.
26. *CEJL*, vol. 1, 231.
27. *The Road to Wigan Pier*, pp. 16-17.
28. Thomas Carlyle, *Past and Present*, (London, 1960) p. 264.
29. '*The Road to Wigan Pier* Diary,' *CEJL*, vol. 1, 177.
30. *The Road to Wigan Pier*, pp. 92-3.
31. Ibid., p. 91.
32. Erik Erikson, op. cit., p. 186.
33. *Coming Up for Air*, pp. 26-7.

34. John Osborne, *Luther* (London, 1961) p. 91.
35. 'Reflections on Gandhi', *CEJL*, vol. 4, 466.
36. 'The Prevention of Literature', *CEJL*, vol. 4, 69.
37. Quoted by Erik Erikson, op. cit., p. 186.
38. *The Road to Wigan Pier*, p. 86.
39. Ibid., p. 79.
40. Rudyard Kipling, 'Independence', in *A Book of Words* (Sussex Edition, 1938) p. 232.
41. *CEJL*, vol. 1, 308.
42. 'The Prevention of Literature', *CEJL*, vol. 4, 60.
43. *Down and Out in Paris and London*, p. 188.

CHAPTER 3

1. George Sabine (ed.), *The Works of Gerrard Winstanley* (New York, 1941) p. 38.
2. 'Looking Back on the Spanish War', *CEJL*, vol. 2, 265-6.
3. Rudyard Kipling, 'The Conversion of Aurelian McGoggin', in *Plain Tales from Hills* (Susses Edition, 1937) p. 154.
4. Rudyard Kipling, 'In the Interests of the Brethren', in *Debits and Credits* (Sussex Edition, 1937) p. 59.
5. *A Clergyman's Daughter*, p. 261.
6. R.H. Tawney, *Religion and the Rise of Capitalism* (London, 1961) p. 229.
7. Ibid., pp. 229-30.
8. John Bunyan, *Pilgrims Progress* (London, 1970) p. 115.
9. 'Rudyard Kipling', *CEJL*, vol. 2, 187.
10. *Burmese Days*, p. 174.
11. 'Culture and Democracy', in *Victory and Vested Interest*, p. 90.
12. Quoted by A.S.P. Woodhouse, *Puritanism and Liberty* (London, 1950) p. 44.
13. 'Looking back on the Spanish War', *CEJL*, vol. 2, 251-2.
14. *CEJL*, vol. 1, 269.
15. *CEJL*, vol. 1, 280.
16. *Homage to Catalonia*, pp. 85, 130.
17. *CEJL*, vol. 4, 203.
18. 'Inside the Whale', *CEJL*, vol. 1, 521-2.
19. Ibid., p. 526.
20. Ibid., p. 500.
21. *CEJL*, vol. 1, 226.
22. 'Inside the Whale', *CEJL*, vol. 1, 526.
23. *The Road to Wigan Pier*, p. 173.
24. Ibid., p. 176.

25. Quoted by R.H. Tawney, op. cit., p. 241
26. Ibid., p. 123.
27. 'The Lion and the Unicorn', *CEJL*, vol. 2, 103-4.
28. *CEJL*, vol. 4, 25.
29. 'Prophecies of Fascism', *CEJL*, vol. 2, 30.
30. *CEJL*, vol. 2, 14.
31. *CEJL*, vol. 4, 480.
32. *The Road to Wigan Pier*, p. 21.
33 R.H.Tawney, op. cit., p. 120.
34. *The Road to Wigan Pier*, pp. 103-4.
35. George Sabine (ed), op. cit., p. 236.
36. *The Road to Wigan Pier*, pp. 143-4.
37. *CEJL*, vol. 3, 99.
38. 'The Lion and the Unicorn', *CEJL* vol. 2, 107.
39. 'Fascism and Democracy', in *The Betrayal of the Left*, ed. Victor Gollancz (London, 1941) p. 215.
40. *CEJL*, vol. 1, 532.
41. *The Road to Wigan Pier*, p. 30.
42. 'Rudyard Kipling', *CEJL*, vol. 2, 184.
43. 'As One Non-Combatant to Another', *CEJL*, vol. 2, 300.
44. *The Road to Wigan Pier*, pp. 127-8.
45. Ibid., p. 100.
46. George Sabine (ed), op. cit., p. 213.
47. A.S.P. Woodhouse, op. cit., p. 43.
48. C.E. Vaughan (ed), *Milton's Areopagitica and other Prose Works*, (London: Everyman, 1927) p. 31.
49. Philip Rieff, 'George Orwell and the post-Liberal Imagination', in *Orwell's Nineteen Eighty-Four, Text, Sources, Criticism*, ed. Howe, p. 234.
50. 'Why I Write', *CEJL*, vol. 1, 3-4.

CHAPTER 4

1. Erik Erikson, *Young Man Luther*, p. 187.
2. Ibid., p. 189.
3. John Osborne, *Luther* (London, 1961) pp. 73-4.
4. *Down and Out in Paris and London*, p. 9.
5. Ibid., pp. 100, 103.
6. Ibid., p. 108.
7. Ibid., p. 17.
8. Ibid., pp. 50-51.
9. Ibid., p. 19.
10. Ibid., p. 19.
11. Ibid., pp. 114-5.

12. Ibid., p. 115.
13. Ibid., p. 113.
14. Ibid., p. 119.
15. Ibid., p. 150.
16. Ibid., p. 161.
17. *The Road to Wigan Pier*, pp. 132-3.
18. Ibid., p. 132.
19. Ibid., p. 133.
20. Nicola Chiaromonte, *The Paradox of History* (London, n.d.) p. 50.
21. *The Road to Wigan Pier*, pp. 129-31.
22. Ibid., p. 134.
23. 'Notes on the Way', *CEJL*, vol. 2, 15.
24. Barbara Everett, *Auden* (London, 1964) p. 71.
25. *The Road to Wigan Pier*, p. 113.
26. Ibid., p. 132.
27. *Down and Out in Paris and London*, p. 115.
28. Ibid., p. 130.
29. Ibid., pp. 166, 177, 146, 128.
30. Ibid., p. 173.
31. 'The Spike', *CEJL*, vol. 1, 37.
32. *The Road to Wigan Pier*, p. 110.
33. Ibid., p. 112.
34. Ibid., p. 113.
35. Ibid., p. 124.
36. Ibid., p. 125.
37. Ibid., p. 137.
38. Ibid., p. 141.
39. *Down and Out in Paris and London*, p. 125.
40. *The Road to Wigan Pier*, p. 136.
41. Ibid., p. 115.
42. 'Such, Such Were the Joys', *CEJL*, vol. 4, 343.
43. Ibid., p. 334.
44. Ibid., p. 334.
45. Ibid., p. 348.
46. Ibid., p. 352.
47. Ibid., pp. 343-4.
48. J.S. Whale, *The Protestant Tradition*, (Cambridge, 1962) p. 24.
49. Ibid., p. 26.
50. 'Such, Such Were the Joys', *CEJL*, vol. 4, 360.
51. Ibid., pp. 340-1.
52. Ibid., pp. 342-3.
53. Ibid., p. 334.
54. Erik Erikson, op. cit., p. 176.

55. 'Such, Such Were the Joys', *CEFL*, vol. 4, 350-1.
56. Erik Erikson, op. cit., pp. 205, 206.
57. *Keep the Aspidistra Flying*, pp. 20–1.
58. *The Road to Wigan Pier*, pp. 15–6.
59. *Down and Out in Paris and London*, p. 179.
60. *Keep the Aspidistra Flying*, p. 100.
61. Ibid., p. 99.
62. Ibid., p. 87.
63. Ibid., pp. 18–9.
64. Ibid., p. 160.
65. Ibid., p. 55.
66. Ibid., p. 217.
67. Ibid., p. 49.
68. Ibid., p. 19.
69. Ibid., p. 207.
70. Ibid., p. 209.
71. Ibid., p. 217.
72. *CEJL*, vol. 1, 530.
73. *Keep the Aspidistra Flying*, p. 226.
74. Ibid., p. 223.
75. Ibid., p. 234.
76. Rudyard Kipling, *Kim* (London, Macmillan Pocket Edition, 1914) pp. 403–4.
77. *Keep the Aspidistra Flying*, p. 255.
78. Ibid., p. 252.
79. Ibid., p. 253.
80. Ibid., p. 254.
81. Ibid., pp. 253–4.
82. Ibid., p. 256.
83. Ibid., pp. 263–4.
84. Ibid., p. 253.
85. Dan Jacobson, 'Orwell's Slumming', in *The World of George Orwell*, ed. Miriam Gross, (London, 1971) p. 49. This is one of the few essays in the collection to suggest that the 'weight of guilt' Orwell talks about in *The Road to Wigan Pier* has 'deeper roots in his own character and history than his spell in the Imperial Police' (p. 49.).

CHAPTER 5

1. 'Notes on the Way', *CEJL*, vol. 2, 15.
2. 'Looking Back on the Spanish War', *CEJL*, vol. 2, 265–6.
3. 'As I please', *CEJL*, vol. 3, 103.
4. Ibid., p. 103.

5. *CEJL*, vol. 1, 383.
6. *Nineteen Eighty-Four*, p. 126.
7. *CEJL*, vol. 3, 100.
8. 'As I Please', *CEJL*, vol. 3, 103.
9. Ibid., p. 103.
10. Ibid., p. 103.
11. Ibid., p. 102.
12. *A Clergyman's Daughter*, p. 258.
13. 'As I Please', *CEJL*, vol. 3, 103.
14. 'Notes on the Way', *CEJL*, vol. 2, 15.
15. 'Rediscovery of Europe' in *The Listener*, (19 Mar 1942) p. 372.
16. In *The Adelphi*, (July, 1934) p. 293.
17. 'Notes on the Way', *CEJL*, vol. 2, 10.
18. J.S. Whale, *The Protestant Tradition*, p. 266.
19. 'Arthur Koestler', *CEJL*, vol. 3, 244.
20. 'Notes on the Way', *CEJL*, vol. 2, 17.
21. *CEJL*, vol. 2, 240.
22. 'Pacifism and the War', *CEJL*, vol. 2, 229.
23. 'Charles Dickens', *CEJL*, vol. 1, 460.
24. *The Road to Wigan Pier*, p. 159.
25. Ibid., p. 155.
26. 'Inside the Whale', *CEJL*, vol. 1, 515.
27. 'Notes on Nationalism', *CEJL*, vol. 3, 365.
28. 'The Prevention of Literature', *CEJL*, vol. 4, 60.
29. Ibid., p. 61.
30. Ibid., p. 63.
31. *CEJL*, vol. 4, 456.
32. 'Notes on the Way', *CEJL*, vol. 2, 17.
33. *CEJL*, vol. 1, 101.
34. *CEJL*, vol. 1, 50.
35. 'Toward European Unity', *CEJL*, vol. 4, 374.
36. 'Why I Write', *CEJL*, vol. 1, 5.
37. 'Notes on the Way', *CEJL*, vol. 2, 18.
38. Malcolm Muggeridge, 'A Knight of the Woeful Countenance', in *The World of George Orwell*, ed. Miriam Gross, p. 167.
39. George Woodcock, *The Crystal Spirit*, (London, 1967) p. 116.
40. *A Clergyman's Daughter*, p. 261.
41. *Poem, CEJL*, vol. 1, 118.
42. *A Clergyman's Daughter*, p. 105.
43. Ibid., p. 220.
44. Ibid., p. 244.
45. Ibid., p. 227.
46. Ibid., p. 50.

47. Ibid., p. 53.
48. Ibid., p. 259.
49. Ibid., p. 258.
50. Ibid., p. 78.

CHAPTER 6

1. 'Culture and Democracy', in *Victory and Vested Interest*, p. 97.
2. 'New Words', *CEJL*, vol. 2, 4.
3. 'Propagandist Critics', in *New English Weekly*, (December, 1936) p. 230.
4. Boris Pasternak, *Dr. Zhivago* (London, 1968) p. 396.
5. 'Literature and Totalitarianism', *CEJL*, vol. 2, 134.
6. 'Inside the Whale', *CEJL*, vol. 1, 525.
7. Ibid., p. 525.
8. Ibid., p. 518.
9. 'Literature and Totalitarianism', *CEJL*, vol. 2, 135.
10. 'Lear, Tolstoy and the Fool', *CEJL*, vol. 4, 294.
11. Ibid., p. 300.
12. William Haller, *The Rise of Puritanism* (New York, 1938) p. 38. *See* also p. 96 ff.
13. *Homage to Catalonia*, p. 7.
14. Ibid., p. 101.
15. Ibid., p. 102.
16. Ibid., pp. 102–3.
17. Ibid., p. 7.
18. 'Looking Back on the Spanish War', *CEJL*, vol. 2, 266.
19. *Homage to Catalonia*, p. 103.
20. *The Listener*, (25 May, 1938) p. 1140.
21. 'The Prevention of Literature', *CEJL*, vol. 4, 61.
22. *Homage to Catalonia*, p. 153.
23. 'Looking Back on the Spanish War,' *CEJL*, vol. 2, 258.
24. Ibid., pp. 258–9.
25. 'The Prevention of Literature', *CEJL*, vol. 4, 63–4.
26. Richard Friedenthal, *Luther*, trans. John Nowell (London, 1970) p. 344.
27. Henry Manning, *The Temporal Mission of the Holy Ghost* (London, 1865) p. 226.
28. Boris Pasternak, *Dr. Zhivago*, p. 18.
29. Ibid., pp. 48–9.
30. Ibid., p. 50.
31. Ibid., p. 18.
32. Ibid., pp. 125, 126.

33. *Keep the Aspidistra Flying*, pp. 40–1.
34. *Animal Farm*, pp. 6, 7.
35. Ibid., pp. 20–1.
36. Ibid., pp. 74, 75, 76.
37. Ibid., p. 75.
38. *Nineteen Eighty-Four*, p. 176.
39. *Coming Up for Air*, pp. 7–8.
40. Ibid., p. 13.
41. Ibid., pp. 73–4.
42. Ibid., pp. 61–2.
43. Ibid., p. 64.
44. Ibid., p. 188.
45. Ibid., pp. 65–6.
46. Ibid., p. 55.
47. Ibid., p. 34.
48. Ibid., p. 74.
49. Ibid., p. 108.
50. Ibid., p. 79.
51. Ibid., p. 231.
52. *The Diaries of Franz Kafka, 1914–1923*, ed. Max Brod, (London, 1949)
    p. 126
53. Erik Erikson, op. cit., pp. 257–8. The context is interesting and
    almost equally apposite:

One may say that man, when looking through a glass darkly, finds
himself in an inner cosmos in which the outlines of three objects
awaken dim nostalgias. One of these is the simple and fervent
wish for a hallucinatory sense of unity with a maternal matrix,
and a supply of benevolently powerful substances; it is symbo-
lized by the affirmative face of charity, graciously inclined, reas-
suring the faithful of the unconditional acceptance of those who
will return to the bosom. In this symbol the split of autonomy is
for ever repaired: shame is healed by unconditional approval,
doubt by the eternal presence of generous provision.

In the centre of the second nostalgia is the paternal voice of
guiding conscience, which puts an end to the simple paradise of
childhood and provides a sanction for energetic action. It also
warns of the inevitability of guilty entanglement, and threatens
with the lightning of wrath. To change the threatening sound of
this voice, if need be by means of partial surrender and manifold

self-castration, is the second imperative demand which enters religious endeavour. At all cost, the Godhead must be forced to indicate that He Himself mercifully planned crime and punishment in order to assure salvation.

Finally, the glass shows the pure self itself, the unborn core of creation, the – as it were, preparental – centre where God is pure nothing: *ein lauter Nichts*, in the words of Angelus Silesius. God is so designated in many ways in Eastern mysticism. This pure self is the self no longer sick with a conflict between right and wrong, not dependent on providers, and not dependent on guides to reason and reality.

54. *Coming Up for Air*, p. 129.
55. Ibid., p. 173.

CHAPTER 7

 1. George Woodcock, *The Crystal Spirit*, p. 89.
 2. Lionel Trilling, 'George Orwell and the Politics of Truth' in *Orwell's Nineteen Eighty-Four. Text, Sources, Criticism*, ed. Howe, p. 221.
 3. *Nineteen Eighty-Four*, pp. 205, 208.
 4. Matthew Hodgart, 'From *Animal Farm* to *Nineteen Eighty-Four*', in *The World of George Orwell*, ed. Miriam Gross, p. 139.
 5. *Nineteen Eighty-Four*, p. 212.
 6. Ibid., p. 68.
 7. Ibid., p. 200.
 8. Ibid., p. 171.
 9. Ibid., p. 205.
10. Ibid., p. 206.
11. Ibid., pp. 67–8.
12. John Osborne, *Luther*, pp. 95–6.
13. *Nineteen Eighty-Four*, p. 136.
14. Ibid., p. 134.
15. Ibid., p. 131.
16. Ibid., p. 120.
17. Ibid., p. 131.
18. Ibid., pp. 119, 177.
19. Ibid., p. 134.
20. Ibid., p. 203.
21. Ibid., pp. 199–200.
22. Ibid., p. 19.
23. Ibid., p. 204.
24. Ibid., p. 82.

25. Ibid., p. 168.
26. Ibid., p. 165.
27. Ibid., pp. 212, 213.
28. Ibid., pp. 166–7.
29. Ibid., p. 17.
30. Ibid., p. 144.
31. Ibid., p. 169.
32. Ibid., p. 170.
33. Ibid., p. 212.
34. Erik Erikson, op. cit., p. 254.
35. *Nineteen Eighty-Four*, p. 19.
36. Ibid., p. 111.
37. Ibid., p. 124.
38. Ibid., p. 130.
39. Ibid., p. 12.
40. Ibid., p. 24.
41. Ibid., p. 192.
42. Ibid., p. 124.
43. Ibid., p. 143.
44. Ibid., p. 205.
45. Ibid., p. 196.
46. Ibid., p. 205.
47. Ibid., pp. 201–2.
48. Ibid., p. 201.
49. Ibid., pp. 202–3.
50. 'Inside the Whale', *CEJL*, vol. 1, p. 495.
51. *Nineteen Eighty-Four*, pp. 218, 219.
52. Ibid., p. 118.
53. Ibid., p. 233.
54. Ibid., p. 238.

Index